Quilts with a Spin

7 New Projects from Piece O' Cake Designs

Becky Goldsmith & Linda Jenkins

C&T PUBLISHING

Text and Artwork © 2005 Becky Goldsmith and Linda Jenkins

Artwork © 2005 C&T Publishing, Inc.

Publisher: Amy Marson

Editorial Director: Gailen Runge

Acquisitions Editor: Jan Grigsby

Editor: Lynn Koolish

Technical Editors: Sara Kate MacFarland, Cynthia Keyes Hilton

Copyeditor/Proofreader: Wordfirm Inc.

Cover Designer: Kristen Yenche

Page Layout Artist: Kirstie L. McCormick

Illustrators: Becky Goldsmith and Tim Manibuson

Production Assistant: Matt Allen

Photography: Luke Mulks, unless otherwise noted

Published by C&T Publishing, Inc., P.O. Box 1456, Lafayette, CA 94549

Front cover: *Pennsylvania Pickle Dish* by Linda Jenkins

Library of Congress Cataloging-in-Publication Data

Goldsmith, Becky

  Quilts with a spin : 7 new projects from Piece O'Cake Designs / Becky

Goldsmith and Linda Jenkins.

     p. cm.

  Includes bibliographical references and index.

  ISBN 1-57120-245-5 (pbk.)

  1. Patchwork--Patterns. 2. Quilting--Patterns. I. Title: Quilts with a

spin, seven new projects from Piece O'Cake Designs. II. Jenkins, Linda,

1943- III. Piece O'Cake Designs. IV. Title.

  TT835.G6548 2005

  746.46'041--dc22

2004018301

Printed in China

10 9 8 7 6 5 4 3 2 1

Table of Contents

Dedication

A book's dedication provides an author with a personal space to say something meaningful about *someone* who has had an impact on her. There are two of us and we each have a dedication to make.

I dedicate this book to my son, Dennis. Dennis was a kind man. He loved life, and even through a long, painful illness, he always kept his sense of humor and took joy in life. He is my inspiration and I know he would have encouraged me and been so proud of my accomplishments. I believe that after his death, God gave me the opportunity to do more than I could ever have dreamed I was capable of. I know Dennis smiles on me and says, "GO, MOM!"

Linda

If a picture tells a story, my dad, Jack Eckroat, was a stitch! I remember him always having an impish grin. He was a good husband to my mom and a good father to us. Dad could fix—or make—anything. I truly believe that much of who I am now came from my dad. He died just before Linda and I started Piece O' Cake, but my mother says she's sure he's looking down and is very proud. I miss him, I remember him, I do my best to keep his memory alive.

Becky

Acknowledgments

We offer a great big thank-you to Lynn Koolish, our editor at C&T. She is forever teaching us new things about writing a good book. She keeps us on our toes, which inspires us to be better authors, and we appreciate it.

Our technical editor, Sara Kate MacFarland, makes sure that we get the details right. It would be nice to be perfect, but we aren't; we're thankful to have her double-checking us. Kirstie McCormick, this book's designer, has given *Quilts with a Spin* its classy appearance. We love the cover that Kristen Yenche designed. Matt Allen, the production assistant, kept everything running smoothly. We thank you all for your excellent efforts.

Many of you know that we design fabric for P&B Textiles. We are thankful for the opportunity that Irwin Bear at P&B has given us. We love using our fabric—and many others made by P&B.

Like all quilters, we like variety! We are grateful to the following companies for sending us many marvelous fabrics that gave our quilts added pizzazz: Westminster Fabrics, Free Spirit Fabrics, Robert Kaufman Fabrics, and Primrose Gradations.

It's important to have a good sewing machine, and we love our Berninas!.

Introduction

This book began with an interest in circular motion—not the kind that makes you dizzy, but rather the visual rhythm that circular designs display.

Don't you want the person viewing your quilt to stop and watch it for a while? A quilt that is entertaining to the eye will stop traffic. Circular designs keep your eyes busy following the interaction of the curved lines. They are fun to look at!

So, feel the *circular* rhythm! Play with color! But most of all—have some fun with these designs!

Basic Supplies

Fabric: All the fabrics used in the quilts in this book are 100% cotton, unless otherwise noted.

Thread: Use cotton thread with cotton fabric. There are many brands to choose from. Try different brands until you find one that works best for you. We like DMC's 50-weight machine-embroidery thread, Mettler's 60-weight machine-embroidery thread, YLI's 60-weight cotton thread, and Aurifil's 50-weight thread.

Batting: We prefer cotton batting. Our favorite is Hobbs Organic Cotton Batting, either with or without scrim.

Needles for hand appliqué: We use a size 11 Hemming & Son milliner's needle. (A milliner's needle and a straw needle are the same thing.) There are many good needles; find the one that fits *your* hand.

Pins: Use ½″ sequin pins to pin your appliqué pieces in place. Use larger flower-head quilting pins to hold the positioning overlay in place.

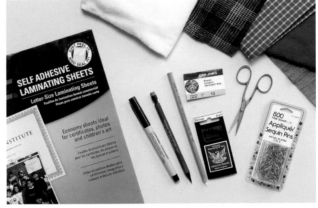

Appliqué supplies

Fusible web: We do not recommend fusible adhesives for use in heirloom quilts. However, if you prefer to fuse and machine stitch your appliqué, use a paper-backed fusible web. Choose the one you like best, and follow the manufacturer's directions.

Nonstick pressing sheet: If you choose to do fusible appliqué, a nonstick pressing sheet will protect your iron and ironing board.

Scissors: Use embroidery-sized scissors for both paper and fabric. Small, sharp scissors are better for intricate cutting.

Rotary cutter, mat, and acrylic ruler: When cutting borders and trimming blocks to size, rotary cutting tools give you the best results.

Pencils: To trace templates onto fabric, we use either a General's brand white charcoal pencil or an Ultimate Mechanical Pencil for Quilters.

Permanent markers: To make the positioning overlay, a Sharpie Ultra Fine Point marker works best on upholstery vinyl.

Clear upholstery vinyl: Use 54″-wide, clear, medium-weight upholstery vinyl to make the positioning overlay. You can usually find this in stores that carry upholstery fabric. Keep the tissue paper that comes with it.

Clear, single-sided, heavy-weight, self-laminating sheets: Use these sheets to make templates; we like the C-Line brand. You can find these sheets at most office supply stores, some warehouse markets, and Viking Office Supply (refer to Resources on page 64).

Sandpaper board: When tracing templates onto fabric, place the fabric on the sandpaper side of the board. Then place the template on the fabric. You'll love the way the sandpaper holds the fabric in place when you trace.

Wooden toothpick: Use a round toothpick to help turn under the turn-under allowance at points and curves. The wood's texture grabs and holds the fabric.

Full-spectrum work light: These lamps give off a bright, natural light. A floor lamp is particularly nice, because you can position it over your shoulder. Appliqué is so much easier when you can see what you are doing.

Machine quilting gloves: These gloves make it easier to hold onto the quilt during machine quilting.

Vellum: We use this crisp, translucent paper for paper piecing. You can find it in quilting, craft, and art stores. Choose white rather than colored vellum.

For Your Information

Fabric Preparation

Cotton has withstood the test of time and is easy to work with. We wash our fabric before using it. This is a good way to test for colorfastness. Also, if the fabric is going to shrink, it does so before being sewn into the quilt. Prewashed fabric is not only easier to work with; it also smells and feels better.

About Our Fabric Requirements

Cotton fabric is usually 40″–44″ wide off the bolt. To be safe, we calculate our fabric requirements based on a 40″ width.

Use the fabric requirements for each quilt as a guide, but remember that the yardage amounts will vary depending on how many fabrics you use and the sizes of pieces you cut. Our measurements allow for both fabric shrinkage and a few errors in cutting.

Seam Allowances

All piecing is designed with ¼″ seam allowances. Be accurate in your piecing so that your quilt tops will fit together properly.

The cutting instructions in this book are mathematically correct. However, variations in the finished size of your quilt top can result from slight differences in seam allowances and the amount of piecing. The measurements provided here should be very close to your actual quilt size, but you should always measure *your* quilt and cut sashings and borders to fit.

Whirlygig

Photo by Sharon Risedorph

Made by Becky Goldsmith, 2003
Finished block size: 16″ x 16″
Finished quilt size: 72″ x 72″

This quilt is just too much fun! Antique whirlygig quilts are often made with two or three colors. Becky combines a rainbow of color with a variety of black-and-white prints to make a quilt that sings.

Materials

This is a scrappy quilt. Use the yardage amounts below as a guide. They will vary with the number of fabrics you use.

Black-and-white prints for block and border backgrounds and pieced arcs: 8 yards

Blue solid for whirlygig appliqué, sashing, and binding fabric: 3⅜ yards

Solid colors for pieced arcs: 1½ yards

Appliqué: A variety of bright fabric scraps to total 2½ yards

Backing and sleeve: 4⅞ yards

Batting: 78″ × 78″

Cutting

Black-and-white prints

Appliqué block backgrounds: Cut 9 squares 13″ × 13″.
Appliqué block corners: Cut 36, using template A.
Pieced arcs: Cut 15 strips 3″ × 40″, then cut into 252 strips 2¼″ × 3″.
Borders: Cut 12″-wide strips in a variety of lengths.
Border corners: Cut 4 squares 12″ × 12″.

Blue fabric

Whirlygig appliqué: Cut 9 squares 13″ × 13″.
Sashing: Cut 24 strips 1½″ × 16½″.
Binding: Cut 1 square 29″ × 29″ to make 2½″-wide continuous bias binding. (Refer to page 58 for instructions.)

Remaining solid fabrics

Pieced arcs: Cut 17 strips 3″ × 40″, then cut into 288 strips 2¼″ × 3″.
Sashing corners: Cut 16 squares 1½″ × 1½″.

Cut fabric for appliqué as needed.

Block Assembly

Refer to pages 52–54 for instructions on making the positioning overlay and preparing the appliqué. The appliqué patterns are on the pullouts at the back of the book.

Appliqué Tips

Use the *cutaway appliqué* technique for the whirlygig. Use the *circle appliqué* technique for the block center. (Refer to pages 56–57 for instructions.)

Block Centers

1. Make 2 templates from the Whirlygig pattern, using template B for the whirlygig blades and template C for the entire block center. Be sure to include the seam allowances in template C.

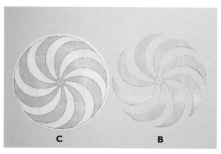

C   B

Make 2 templates.

2. Notice that the whirlygig blades are connected at the center of template B. It is easier, and the results are better, if you use cutaway appliqué to sew the block. Carefully trace around the whirlygig template onto the blue fabric.

Carefully trace around the template.

3. Finger-press all edges that will be appliquéd. Don't cut the fabric apart!

Finger-press the whirlygig.

4. Center the blue whirlygig over a black-and-white background. Baste the blades of the whirlygig in place.

Baste the blades in place.

5. Appliqué the whirlygig, using the cutaway appliqué technique.

Trim excess fabric.

Appliqué.

6. Press the block on the wrong side. Place the overlay over the block so you can see where the center circle will fall. Carefully trim the excess blue fabric in the center of the block, but don't trim too much!

7. Appliqué the center circle to the block. Press the block from the wrong side.

8. Use a positioning pin to center template C over the block. Trace around the template, and trim the excess fabric on the drawn line.

Center template C over the block.

Carefully trace around circle.

Trim excess fabric.

Completed block

Pieced Arcs

Refer to pages 60–61 for instructions on paper piecing the arcs.

1. Make 36 copies of the arc pattern E on vellum.

2. Sew the arcs.

Whirlygig Blocks

Refer to page 62 for instructions on sewing curves.

1. Use template A to cut out 36 block corners.

2. Place the block centers, pieced arcs, and block corners on your design wall. Move them around until you are happy with their placement. This is an important step—don't skip it!

3. Sew the block corners to their respective arcs. Always work with the concave side up. Press.

4. Carefully remove the paper from the arcs.

5. Sew together 4 corner/arc units to make a block.

Sew 4 corner units together.

6. Pin the corner/arc units to the block center. First match the seams to the pressed-in centering grid lines, then pin between them. Pin frequently. Keep the concave sides up.

Pin the corner/arc units to the block center.
Match seams. Pin frequently.

7. Sew the block together.

Sew the block together.

8. Press the seams away from the block center.

Press seams away from block center.

Borders

Refer to pages 52–54 for making the positioning overlay and preparing the appliqué. Appliqué patterns are on the pullouts at the back of the book. Enlarge patterns as noted.

Appliqué Tips

Use the *circle appliqué* technique for the circles. Use the *off-the-block construction* technique to create the layered flowers and stars. Use *cutaway appliqué* for stars. (Refer to pages 56–57 for instructions.)

Quilts with a Spin

In true quilting tradition, Becky used the fabric she had for the borders. There is no pattern to it, and the fabric strips that make up the border backgrounds are random in length.

1. Place your blocks, sashing, and sashing corners on your design wall.

2. Arrange 12″-wide pieces of border fabric around the edges of the quilt.

3. When you are happy with the arrangement, sew the border strips together. Make 4 border backgrounds 12″ × 54″.

4. Place the 4 border corner backgrounds on your design wall.

5. Make the border appliqué templates.

6. Make a pattern for the border. The same pattern is used for all 4 borders. Draw a 10″ × 52″ rectangle on a long piece of paper. Refer to the Quilt Assembly Diagram for appliqué shape placement in the border. Place the templates on the paper as shown in the diagram. Trace around them. Make your positioning overlay from this pattern.

7. Make a pattern for the border corners the same way. The same pattern is used for all 4 border corners. Draw a 10″ × 10″ square on a piece of paper.

8. Audition all of the border appliqué pieces on the design wall.

9. Appliqué the borders.

10. When the appliqué is complete, press the borders on the wrong side. Trim the borders to 10½″ × 52½″.

11. Appliqué the border corners.

12. When the appliqué is complete, press the border corners on the wrong side. Trim the border corners to 10½″ × 10½″.

Quilt Assembly

Refer to the Quilt Assembly Diagram (page 12) for quilt construction.

1. Sew 3 appliqué blocks together, with sashing strips between them, to form a row. Sew a sashing strip to each end. Make 3 rows. Press the seams toward the sashing strips.

2. Sew 3 sashing strips, with a sashing corner between them, to form a row. Sew a sashing corner to each end. Make 4 rows. Press the seams toward the sashing corners.

3. Sew the rows of blocks and sashing rows together. Press toward the sashing rows.

4. Sew the side borders to the quilt. Press toward the inner sashing.

5. Sew the appropriate border corner block to each end of the top and bottom borders. Sew the top and bottom borders to the quilt. Press toward the sashing.

6. Finish the quilt. (Refer to page 55 for instructions.)

Quilt Assembly Diagram

Quilts with a Spin

Pennsylvania Pickle Dish

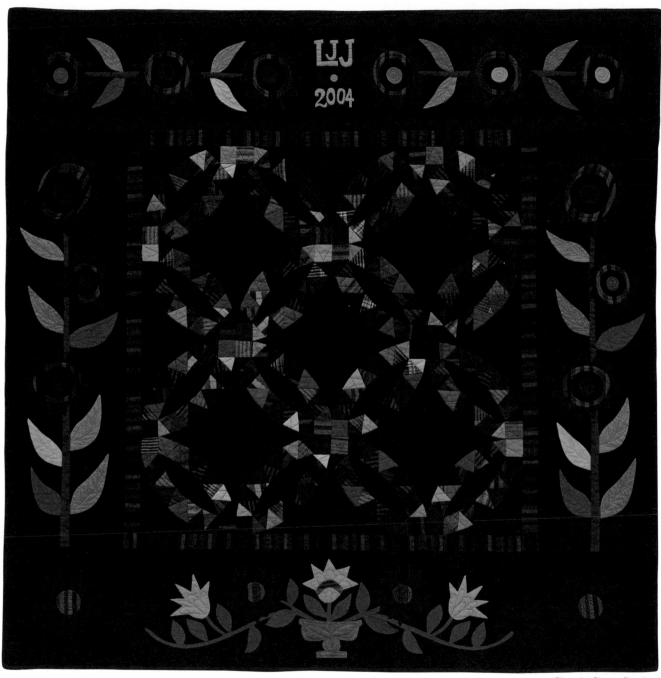

Photo by Sharon Risedorph

Made by Linda Jenkins, 2004

Finished quilt center: 36″ × 36″

Finished quilt size: 60″ × 60″

Linda was after a folk-art attitude in this quilt—and she got it! She used an interesting mix of hand-dyed solids and woven plaids to make this quilt sparkle. The pickle dish rings are a splash of color on the royal blue background. Three different border designs pull it all together perfectly.

Materials

This is a scrappy quilt. Use the yardage amounts below as a guide; they will vary with the number of fabrics you use.

Royal blue fabric for the background in the quilt center and border, and the binding: 5½ yards

Colorful solid fabric for the outside of the arcs and arc corners: 1¾ yards

Colorful striped or plaid fabric for the inside of the arcs and arc corners: 1¼ yards

Striped fabric for the inner border: ⅓ yard

Appliqué: A variety of bright fabric scraps to total 4½ yards

Red solid for the zigzags in the top border: ⅜ yard

Backing and sleeve: 4 yards

Batting: 66″ × 66″

Cutting

Royal blue fabric
Template C: Cut 16.
Template D: Cut 5.
Template E: Cut 4.
Template F: Cut 4.

Royal blue fabric (continued)
Outer side borders: Cut 2 strips 13″ × 42″.
Outer top and bottom borders: Cut 2 strips 13″ × 62″.
Binding: Cut 1 square 29″ × 29″ to make 2½″-wide continuous bias binding. (Refer to page 58 for instructions.)

Colorful solid fabric
Triangles on the outside of the arcs: Cut 14 strips 3″ × 40″, then cut 128 pieces 2½″ × 3″ and 64 pieces 3½″ × 3″.
Arc corners: Cut 16 squares 2¼″ × 2¼″.

Colorful striped or plaid fabric
Triangles on the inside of the arcs: Cut 13 strips 3″ × 40″, then cut 160 pieces 2½″ × 3″.
Arc corners: Cut 16 squares 2¼″ × 2¼″.

Striped fabric
Inner side borders: Cut 2 strips 2″ × 36½″.
Inner top and bottom borders: Cut 2 strips 2″ × 39½″.

Red solid
Cut 4 strips 2¼″ × 40″, then sew together as needed to make 2 strips 2¼″ × 62″.

Cut fabric for appliqué as needed.

Block Assembly

Pieced Arcs

Refer to pages 60–61 for instructions on paper piecing the arcs. Patterns are on the pullouts at the back of the book.

1. Make 16 copies of the arc pattern A on vellum.

2. Sew the arcs.

3. Make 16 copies of the arc pattern B on vellum. Notice that the arc corners will be sewn to either end of these arcs. Corner 1 is a solid fabric, and corner 13 is a striped or plaid fabric.

4. Sew the arcs.

5. The small dots on templates C, D, E, and F indicate where seams must be matched. Make a small hole through these dots. Place a chalk mark through these holes onto the wrong side of the pieced arcs. Do not use a permanent marker.

6. The arc foundation papers are also marked with small dots that indicate where seams must be matched. Pierce the arc foundations at each dot, and place a small mark on the wrong side of the fabric.

7. Gently remove the paper from all arcs.

Pickle Dish Blocks

Refer to page 62 for instructions on sewing curves.

1. The small dots on templates C, D, E, and F indicate where seams must be matched. Make a small hole through these dots. Place a mark through these holes onto the wrong side of the background pieces. Do not use a permanent marker.

Positioning Pin Tips

Use a positioning pin to match the dots on the arcs and background pieces. Find the center points that must be matched. Place the fabrics right sides together. Push a pin through the points that must match up. This first pin is your positioning pin. Make sure that your pin goes through both marked dots. Hold the positioning pin perpendicular to the fabric and place a second pin very close to the positioning pin to attach the two fabrics. Repeat for each end of the pieces you are pinning.

We leave the positioning pins in place as long as possible, removing them only when they get in the way of sewing.

2. Sew pieced arc A to background piece C. Use positioning pins to align the seam ends, as marked on the wrong side of your fabric. Sew with the arc side up. Press to the background. Repeat for all A arcs.

Sew arc **A** to background **C**. Use positioning pins to match ends.

3. Sew pieced arc B to the other side of background C. Use positioning pins to align the seam ends, as marked on the wrong side of your fabric. Sew with the arc side up. Press to the background. Repeat for all B arcs.

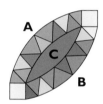

Sew arc **B** to the other side of background **C**. Use positioning pins to match ends.

4. Arrange all of the arc units and the pickle dish background pieces on your design wall so that the solid and striped corners alternate.

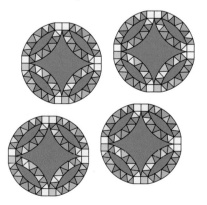

Arrange the arc units and the backgrounds so that solid and striped corners alternate.

5. Pay attention to the position of the solid and striped/plaid corners. Sew a completed arc unit to background piece D. Match the centers and seam ends. Sew with the background piece on top. Press to the background.

6. Sew an arc unit to the other side of background piece D. Press to the background.

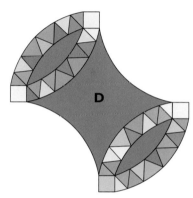

Sew an arc unit to opposite sides of background **D**. Use positioning pins to match ends.

7. Sew an arc to each of the remaining 2 sides of background D. Press to the background. Repeat to make 4 round Pickle Dish blocks.

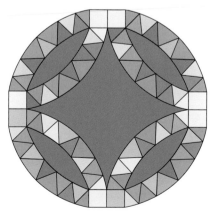

Sew an arc unit to the remaining sides of background **D**. Repeat to make 4 round blocks.

Set the Blocks Together

Refer to the Quilt Center Assembly Diagram for construction.

The trick to setting these round blocks together is to continue matching the centers and to use positioning pins. Sew with the concave side up as much as possible. Use as many pins as necessary to hold the seams in position as you sew. Sew slowly. Think round thoughts!

1. Sew a corner background E to each round Pickle Dish block. Press to the background.

2. Sew the upper left block to the lower right block, with a background D between them. Press to the background.

3. Sew a background F to each side of the upper right block. Press to the background.

4. Sew a background F to each side of the lower left block. Press to the background.

5. Sew the upper right corner to the center row of blocks. Press to the background.

6. Sew the lower left corner to the quilt. Press to the background.

Quilt Center Assembly Diagram

Border Assembly

Refer to pages 52–54 for instructions on making the positioning overlay and preparing the appliqué. Border patterns are on the pullouts at the back of the book. Enlarge patterns as noted.

Appliqué Tips

Use the *circle appliqué* technique for the circles in the flowers. Use *cutaway appliqué* for stems and leaves in the bottom border and between the points on the flowers. (Refer to pages 56–57 for instructions.)

Appliqué Tips

The template for the zigzag strips on the top border is 60 inches long. Tape the paper copies together, being careful to keep them straight. Overlap lengths of laminate on top of the paper template. Trace the zigzag on the red fabric strips. Do not cut out the points! Finger-press and position the strips on the border. Baste them in place. Use the *cutaway appliqué* technique when sewing the points.

1. Place the quilt center and inner borders on your design wall.

2. Place the border backgrounds on your design wall.

3. Audition all of the border appliqué pieces on the design wall.

4. Linda wanted to include her initials and the year on her quilt. This will be a more meaningful addition to your quilt if your initials are in your own handwriting. Just be sure that your initials and the date fit the space on the pattern.

5. Appliqué the borders.

6. When the appliqué is complete, press the borders on the wrong side.

7. Trim the side borders to 11″ × 39½″.

8. Trim the top and bottom borders to 11″ × 60½″.

Quilt Assembly

Refer to the Quilt Assembly Diagram for quilt construction.

1. Sew the side inner borders to the quilt center. Press to the inner border.

2. Sew the top and bottom inner borders to the quilt center. Press to the inner border.

3. Sew the side borders to the quilt. Press to the inner border.

4. Sew the top and bottom borders to the quilt. Press to the inner border.

5. Finish the quilt. (Refer to page 55 for instructions.)

Quilt Assembly Diagram

Empress Feathers

Photo by Sharon Risedorph

Made by Becky Goldsmith, 2003

Finished center block: 30″ x 30″

Finished quilt size: 66″ x 66″

Becky drew inspiration for this quilt from many different antique Princess Feather quilts. She had fun breaking the block apart around the outer edges. Don't the feathers look a little bit like ocean waves breaking on the beach?

Materials

This is a scrappy quilt. Use the yardage amounts below as a guide; they will vary with the number of fabrics you use. The appliqué pieces are big and use more fabric than you'd expect!

Yellow fabrics for the backgrounds: 4½ yards
Red appliqué fabrics: 5 yards (pieces cut on bias)
Teal appliqué fabrics: 4 yards (pieces cut on bias)
Green appliqué fabric: ⅛ yard
Floral print fabric for appliqué and binding: 1½ yards
Backing and sleeve: 4½ yards
Batting: 72″ × 72″

Cutting

Yellow fabric

Center appliqué block backgrounds: Cut 4 squares 17″ × 17″.

Side appliqué block backgrounds: Cut 8 rectangles 17″ × 20″.

Corner appliqué block backgrounds: Cut 4 squares 20″ × 20″.

Floral print fabric

Binding: Cut 1 square 29″ × 29″ to make 2½″-wide continuous bias binding. (Refer to page 58 for instructions.)

Cut fabric for appliqué as needed.

Note: The feathers (appliqué pattern A) and feather veins (appliqué pattern B) are cut on the bias.

Background Tips

We recommend auditioning the background fabrics on your design wall. It's a good idea to first cut all 16 pieces 20″ × 20″ square. Then audition them before cutting each piece to its appropriate size. In the long run, this saves more fabric than it wastes.

Block Assembly

Pieced Backgrounds

1. Place the backgrounds on your design wall. Move them around until you are happy with their placement.

2. Sew the center backgrounds together into a Four-Patch block.

3. Sew the side backgrounds together into pairs.

Center Block

The appliqué patterns are on the pull-outs at the back of the book.

Refer to pages 52–54 for instructions on making the positioning overlay and preparing the appliqué.

Note: This block is very big. It is actually easier to work with a positioning overlay that is not full size. Trace the pattern for one-quarter of the block plus the block center.

Appliqué Tips

Use the *off-the-block construction* and *cutaway appliqué* techniques for the veins in the feathers. Use the *cutaway appliqué* technique for the edges of the feathers, and use the *circle appliqué* technique for the circles. (Refer to pages 56–57 for instructions.)

1. Audition all of the appliqué pieces on the design wall.

2. Match the seamlines with the centerlines drawn on your overlay. Rotate your overlay as necessary.

3. Appliqué the center block. Appliqué the diagonal feathers (patterns A and B) before filling in the feathers that lie over the seams.

4. When the appliqué is complete, press the block on the wrong side. Trim the block to 30½" × 30½".

Side Blocks

Note: Be aware that some of the appliqué pieces in the side and corner blocks fall very close to the outer edge of the block. Do not let your appliqué migrate out of position.

1. Match the seamline with one of the centerlines on your overlay. Press a second line into your background perpendicular to the seam and 4" from the outer edge of the side block backgrounds. The pressed line matches the other center line on the overlay.

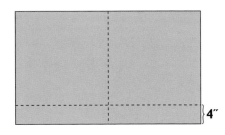

Press a centering line perpendicular to the seam and 4" in from the outer edge.

2. Appliqué the side blocks. Appliqué the diagonal feathers first, then fill in the feathers that lie over the seams. You do not need to appliqué beyond the edge of the block.

3. When the appliqué is complete, press the block on the wrong side.

4. Trim the block to 18½" × 30½". Be sure to leave ⅜" between the edge of appliqué piece C and the cut edge of the block.

Corner Blocks

1. Press a line 4" from one outer edge of the corner block backgrounds. Press a second line perpendicular to the first line and 4" from the outer edge. The pressed lines match the center lines on the overlay.

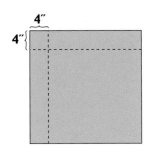

Press 2 lines 4" in from the outer edge.

2. Appliqué the corner blocks. Appliqué the diagonal feathers first. You do not need to appliqué beyond the edge of the block.

3. When the appliqué is complete, press the block on the wrong side.

4. Trim the block to 18½" × 18½". Be sure to leave ⅜" between the edge of appliqué piece C and the cut edge of the block.

Quilt Assembly

Refer to the Quilt Assembly Diagram for quilt construction.

1. Sew a side block to each side of the center block. Press toward the center.

2. Sew a corner block to each side of 2 remaining side blocks. Press toward the corners.

3. Sew the rows together. Press toward the center.

4. Appliqué pieces G, H, and I in place.

5. Finish the quilt. (Refer to page 55 for instructions.)

Quilt Assembly Diagram

Whig's Defeat

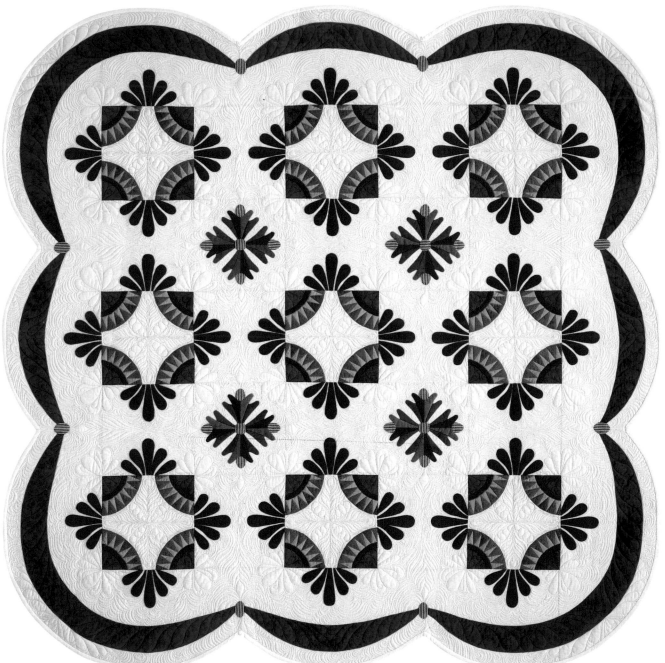

Photo by Sharon Risedorph

Made by Linda Jenkins,
quilted by Linda V. Taylor, 2004
Finished block size: 10″ × 10″
Finished quilt size: 70″ × 70″

Linda made this lovely traditional quilt to top her bed. Linda V. Taylor added stupendous quilting in the open areas. The color and pattern of the appliqué, together with the texture of the quilted feathers, make this a very special quilt!

Materials

Off-white fabrics for block backgrounds, border, and binding: 6½ yards

Dark pink fabric for appliqué and pieced arcs: 1½ yards

Light pink fabric for appliqué: 1⅛ yards

Dark green fabric for appliqué, block corners, and border swags: 2½ yards

Light green fabric for pieced arcs: ¾ yard

Pink striped fabric for appliqué: ¼ yard

Backing and sleeve: 4⅞ yards

Batting: 76″ × 76″

Cutting

Off-white fabrics

Top and bottom border backgrounds: Cut 2 strips lengthwise 12″ × 74″.

Side border backgrounds: Cut 2 strips lengthwise 12″ × 52″.

Appliqué block backgrounds: Cut 16 squares 12″ × 12″.

Template D: Cut 36.

Binding: Cut 1 square 29″ × 29″ to make 2½″-wide continuous bias binding. (Refer to page 58 for instructions.)

Dark pink fabric

Template B: Cut 36.

Templates E, F, G, FR, and GR: Cut 36 each.

Oak leaf J: Cut 2 strips 2½″ × 40″, then cut 16 rectangles 2½″ × 4½″.

Light pink fabric

Pieced arc A: Cut 12 strips 2½″ × 40″, then cut 252 rectangles 1¾″ × 2½″.

Oak leaf J: Cut 2 strips 2½″ × 40″, then cut 16 rectangles 2½″ × 4½″.

Dark green fabric

Template C: Cut 36.

Oak leaf H: Cut 16.

Side border swag M: Cut 4.

Corner border swag L: Cut 4.

Light green fabric

Pieced arc A: Cut 9 strips 2½″ × 40″, then cut 216 rectangles 1½″ × 2½″.

Pink striped fabric

Oak leaf I: Cut 24. Use 16 in the Oak Leaf blocks and 8 in the border.

Circle K: Cut 4. Use in the Oak Leaf blocks.

Block Assembly

Pieced Blocks

Refer to pages 60–61 for instructions on paper piecing the arcs. Refer to page 62 for instructions on sewing curves.

1. Make 36 copies of arc pattern A on vellum.

2. Cut out the copies, following the outer dashed lines.

3. Sew the arcs.

4. Sew an off-white outside corner D to each arc. Always work with the concave side up. Press away from the arc.

5. Carefully remove the paper from the arcs.

6. Sew a dark pink accent B to each dark green inside corner C. Always work with the concave side up. Press toward the accent strip.

7. Sew the 2 halves of the unit together. Always work with the concave side up. Note that the pieced arc will stay in place better if you use a pin at each seam along the arc. Press away from the pieced arc.

8. Sew 4 blocks together to make the larger pieced block. Press seams in alternate directions.

Appliqué Blocks

Refer to pages 52–54 for instructions on making the positioning overlay and preparing the appliqué. The appliqué patterns for the swags are on the pull-outs at the back of the book.

Petal Blocks

1. Make templates and an overlay for the Petal blocks.

2. Appliqué your blocks. When the appliqué is complete, press the blocks on the wrong side. Trim each block to a $10\frac{1}{2}'' \times 10\frac{1}{2}''$ square.

Oak Leaf Blocks

1. Make templates and an overlay for the Oak Leaf blocks.

2. Sew a dark pink rectangle to a light pink rectangle. Repeat for all 16 light and dark pink units.

3. Center the Oak Leaf block template over the sewn unit, and trace appliqué shape J.

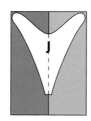

4. Trace appliqué shapes H and I as directed in the cutting instructions.

5. Appliqué your blocks. When the appliqué is complete, press the blocks on the wrong side. Trim each block to a $10\frac{1}{2}'' \times 10\frac{1}{2}''$ square.

Borders and Quilt Assembly

Refer to the Quilt Assembly Diagram for quilt construction.

1. Set the blocks together.

Set blocks together.

2. Be sure to position the groups of petals correctly on each border. The center of each petal group should align with the center of the adjacent pieced block. Measure the distance between the centers of the blocks on your quilt. They should be at or near 20″ apart. Press a line to mark the center of each petal group on each border background in addition to the lengthwise center line.

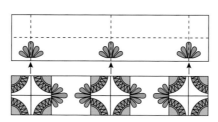

Align petal groups with the center of the adjacent pieced block.

Note: The finished edges at the base of each petal should be 1″ away from the cut edge of the border.

3. The border backgrounds are not yet trimmed to size, so don't appliqué the petals too close to the edge of the border. The *finished* end of each petal should be 1″ from the cut edge of the border background.

4. Appliqué the petals in the borders.

5. After appliquéing the petal groups, press the borders on the wrong side.

6. Trim the side borders to $52\frac{1}{2}''$. Measure $5\frac{1}{4}''$ from the lengthwise center of the border to the inside edge and trim the excess fabric. **Do not trim the outer edge of the side border strips.** Sew the side borders to the quilt.

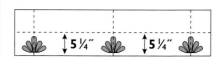

7. Trim the top and bottom borders to $72\frac{1}{2}''$. Measure $5\frac{1}{4}''$ from the lengthwise center of the border to the inside edge and trim the excess fabric. **Do not trim the outer edge of the top and bottom border strips.** Sew the top and bottom borders to the quilt.

8. Use template M to trace 4 side border swags.

9. Use template L to trace 4 corner border swags. Note that template L is one-half of the corner swag. Trace around three sides of the template, but don't trace the flat end. Turn the template upside down and match the flat ends. Then trace the other half of the swag.

Border Swag Tips

Use a modified *cutaway appliqué* technique for the swags. Cut your seam allowance ½″ wide and trim it to ³⁄₁₆″ as you go. This will make it easier to position the swags on the borders while still protecting the long outer edges of the swags.

Use the *circle appliqué* technique for the oval oak leaf berries and the ovals in the swags. (Refer to pages 56–57 for instructions.)

10. No matter how accurate we are, our quilts are not always *exactly* the size the pattern calls for. Because of this, the placement of the swags will vary from quilt to quilt. Make sure the ends of the swags line up with the *centers* of the adjacent petal blocks and are 4″ from the body of the quilt. Finger-press each swag. Then take your time and carefully place the swags on your quilt. Baste them in place. Appliqué the border.

11. Press the quilt on the wrong side. Trim the outer edges of the quilt, following the shape of the swag. Leave 1″ or more of background beyond the edge of the swag.

12. Finish the quilt. (Refer to page 55 for instructions.)

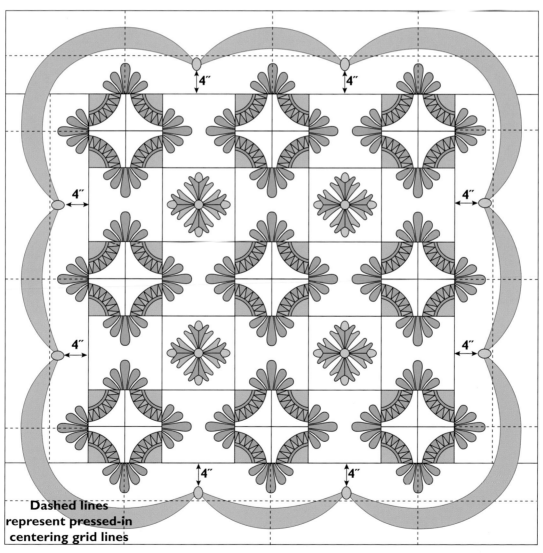

Quilt Assembly Diagram

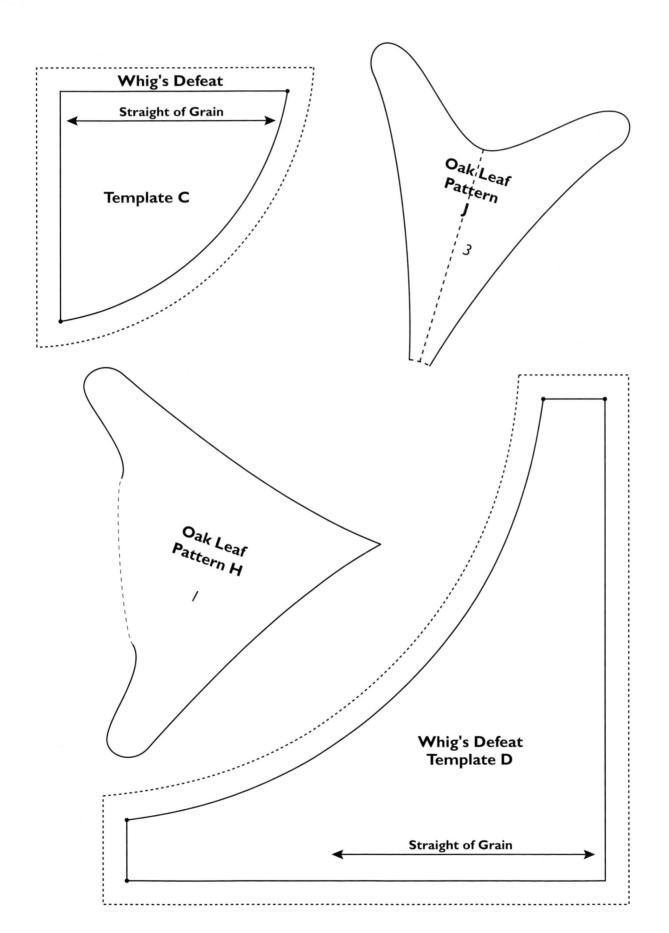

Whig's Defeat

Straight of Grain

Template C

Oak Leaf Pattern J

3

Oak Leaf Pattern H

1

Whig's Defeat Template D

Straight of Grain

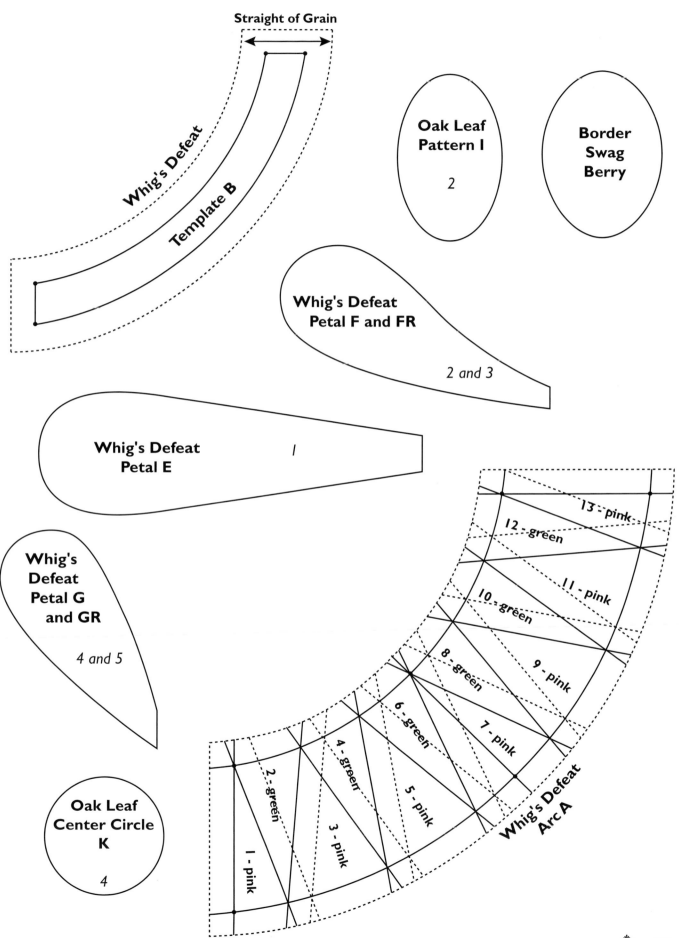

Straight of Grain

Whig's Defeat
Template B

Oak Leaf
Pattern I

2

Border
Swag
Berry

Whig's Defeat
Petal F and FR

2 and 3

Whig's Defeat
Petal E

I

Whig's
Defeat
Petal G
and GR

4 and 5

Oak Leaf
Center Circle
K

4

13 - pink
12 - green
11 - pink
10 - green
9 - pink
8 - green
7 - pink
6 - green
5 - pink
4 - green
3 - pink
2 - green
1 - pink

Whig's Defeat
Arc A

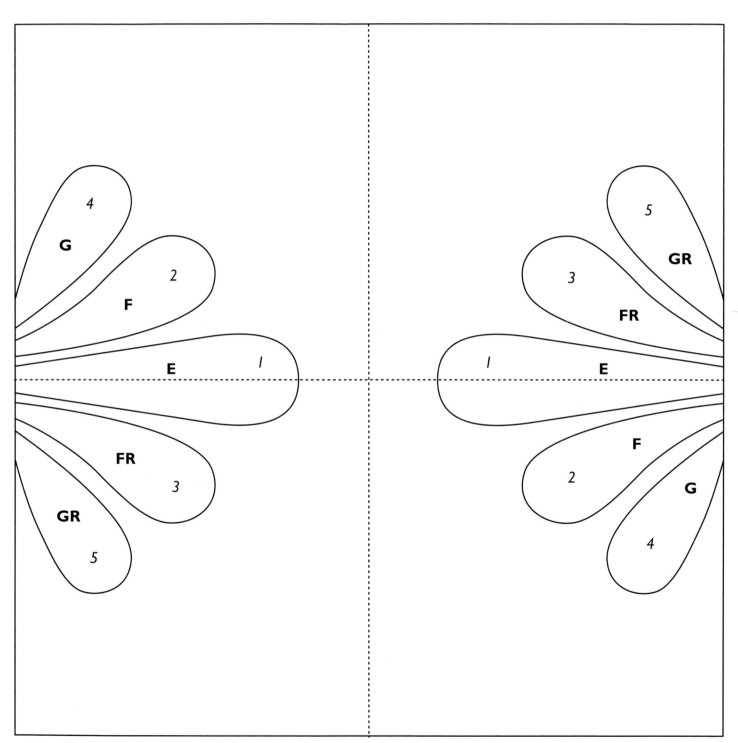

Whig's Defeat Petal Block
Enlarge the block 135% to a 10″ x 10″ square.

Whig's Defeat Oak Leaf Block
Enlarge the block 135% to a 10″ x 10″ square.

Everyday Best

Made by Becky Goldsmith, 2003

Finished block size: 16″ × 16″

Finished quilt size: 73″ × 73″

*Don't these blocks make you think of dishes? Not your grandmother's formal china dishes. No, these are the best dishes that you would use every day! Look closely and you'll see that Becky used **lots** of dots in combination with florals and stripes to make this very perky quilt.*

Materials

This is a scrappy quilt. Use the yardage amounts below as a guide; they will vary with the number of fabrics you use.

Becky ran out of some fabric when she got to the border backgrounds. Rather than stop, she got creative and used fabric from her stash to finish the borders.

Light fabrics for blocks: ⅔ yard
Light/medium fabrics for blocks, inner border, and
  sashing: 5¾ yards
Dark fabrics for blocks: 3⅔ yards
Dark green for vines and stems: ⅓ yard
Appliqué: A variety of fabric scraps to total 2¼ yards
Binding: 1 yard
Backing and sleeve: 5 yards
Batting: 78″ × 78″

Cutting

Light fabrics
Pieced arcs A: Cut 1 strip 3¾″ × 40″, then cut into 20 pieces 2″ × 3¾″.
Pieced arcs B and C: Cut 2 strips 3½″ × 40″, then cut into 44 pieces 1¾″ × 3½″.
Outer corners of center block: Cut 4 pieces using template D.

Light/medium fabrics
Pieced arcs A: Cut 4 strips 3¾″ × 40″, then cut into 72 pieces 2″ × 3¾″.
Pieced arcs B and C: Cut 16 strips 3½″ × 40″, then cut into 352 pieces 1¾″ × 3½″.
Inside corners of the remaining blocks: Cut 12 pieces, using template D.
Sashing: Cut 12 strips 4½″ × 16½″.
Sashing corners: Cut 4 squares 4½″ × 4½″.
Inner side borders: Cut 3 strips 3½″ × 40″, then seam together to make 2 strips 3½″ × 56½″.
Inner top and bottom borders: Cut 4 strips 3½″ × 40″, then seam together to make 2 strips 3½″ × 75″.
Outer side borders: Cut 3 strips 7″ × 40″, then seam together to make 2 strips 7″ × 58½″.

Light/medium fabrics (continued)
Outer top and bottom borders: Cut 4 strips 7″ × 40″, then seam together to make 2 strips 7″ × 77″.

Dark fabrics
Pieced arcs A: Cut 4 strips 3¾″ × 40″, then cut into 72 pieces 2″ × 3¾″.
Pieced arcs B and C: Cut 18 strips 3½″ × 40″, then cut into 396 pieces 1¾″ × 3½″.
Outer corners of the outer blocks: Cut 20 pieces using template D.

Dark green
Borders: Cut 7 strips 1¼″ × 40″, then seam together to make:
2 strips 1¼″ × 56½″ for the straight vines in the side borders.
2 strips 1¼″ × 75″ for the straight vines in the top and bottom borders.

Binding
Cut 1 square 32″ × 32″ to make 2½″-wide continuous bias binding. (Refer to page 58 for instructions.) Or do what Becky did and make your square from wide strips of green fabric used in the quilt.

Cut fabric for appliqué as needed.

A word about fabric choices:

Dotted fabric can be very visually active. A black dot on a white background (high contrast) is an example of fabric that is visually active. As the contrast goes down, the fabric becomes less active, or calmer. If all of your fabrics are very active it will be hard to see the pattern in the quilt. Be sure to use both calm and active fabrics in your quilt.

The instructions refer to light, light/medium, and dark value fabrics. In this quilt, value placement is as important as color placement. The very lightest fabrics are used sparingly in the blocks. You will have many fabrics that could be either light or medium depending on where in the quilt they are used. The darks should obviously be darker than the other fabrics.

Block Assembly

Pieced Arcs

Refer to pages 60–61 for instructions on paper piecing the arcs.

1. Make 36 copies of arc patterns A, B, and C on vellum.

2. Cut out the copies, following the outer dashed lines.

3. Sew the arcs.

Assemble the Blocks

Refer to page 62 for instructions on sewing curves. Corner template D is on the pullout at the back of the book. Enlarge as noted.

1. Sort the block corners (cut from template D) into 4 light, 12 light/medium, and 20 dark block corners. The lightest are at the center of the quilt; the darkest are to the outside.

2. Place the block arcs and corners on your design wall. Move them around until you are happy with their placement. This is an important step—don't skip it!

3. Sew a D corner to its respective C arc. Always work with the concave side up. Press.

4. Carefully remove the paper from the arc.

5. Sew the C/D unit to the B arc. Pin as often as needed. Sew with the concave side up. Press.

6. Carefully remove the paper from the arc.

7. Sew the B/C/D units to the A arc. Pin as often as needed. Sew with the concave side up. Press.

8. Carefully remove the paper from the arc.

9. Repeat for all arcs and corners.

10. Sew 4 units together to form a block.

Borders

Refer to pages 52–54 for instructions on making the positioning overlay and preparing the appliqué. Patterns are on the pullouts at the back of the book. Enlarge patterns as noted.

Appliqué Tips

Use the *cutaway appliqué* technique for the stems. Use the *circle appliqué* technique for the center of the block and the flowers. (Refer to pages 56–57 for instructions.)

Because the blocks are heavily pieced, you should measure *your* blocks before cutting your inner border strips. Be careful not to stretch the blocks as you work with them.

1. Place the blocks on your design wall.

2. Use template E to cut a circle for the center of each block.

3. Arrange the sashing strips and corner squares around the blocks.

4. Cut the border backgrounds and place them on your design wall.

5. Construct 2 strips $1\frac{1}{4}'' \times 56\frac{1}{2}''$ for the straight vine on each side border.

6. Construct 2 strips $1\frac{1}{4}'' \times 75''$ for the straight vine on the top and bottom borders.

7. Make border templates.

8. Make a pattern for the top and bottom borders. The same pattern is used for both top and bottom borders. Draw a $9\frac{1}{2}'' \times 75''$ rectangle on a long piece of paper. Refer to the positioning guide on the pullout and the photo of the quilt for appliqué shape placement. Place the templates on the paper as shown in the positioning guide. Trace around them. Make your positioning overlay from this pattern.

9. Make a pattern for the side borders in the same way. For the side borders, draw a $9\frac{1}{2}'' \times 58''$ rectangle. The same pattern is used for both side borders.

10. Audition all of the border appliqué pieces on the design wall.

11. Appliqué the E circles in the centers of the blocks.

12. Appliqué the side, top, and bottom outer border strips. Press these strips on the wrong side. Trim the inside edge 3″ from the horizontal center. **Don't trim the outer edge until all the borders are sewn to the quilt and the appliqué is complete.** Trim the side outer borders to 56½″. Trim the top and bottom outer borders to 75″.

Quilt Assembly

Refer to the Quilt Assembly Diagram (page 34) for quilt construction.

1. Sew 3 blocks together to form a row. Make 3 rows. Press seams in alternate directions.

2. Sew a sashing strip to each end of the block rows. Press seams in alternate directions.

3. Sew the top sashing strips together to form a row. Sew a corner square to each end of this row. Press in alternate directions.

4. Sew the bottom sashing strips together to form a row. Sew a corner square to each end of this row. Press in alternate directions.

5. Sew the rows together.

6. Sew a side inner border to the quilt. Press toward the inner border. Appliqué your pieces over the inner border and the adjacent sashing. Be careful not to stretch the edges of the quilt. Repeat for the other side inner border.

7. When the side inner border appliqué is complete, press it on the wrong side. Trim the side inner borders 2¼″ from the seamline.

8. Sew a 1¼″ × 56½″ dark green stem strip to each side inner border. Press toward the stem.

9. Sew a side outer border to each side of the quilt. Press toward the stem.

10. Sew the top inner border background to the quilt. Press toward the inner border. Appliqué the pieces over the inner border and the adjacent sashing. Be careful not to stretch the edges of the quilt. Repeat for the bottom inner border.

11. When the appliqué is complete, press it on the wrong side. Trim the inner borders to 2¼″ from the seamline.

12. Sew a 1¼″ × 75″ dark green stem strip to the top and bottom inner borders. Press toward the stem.

13. Sew the top and bottom outer borders to the quilt. Press toward the stem.

14. Appliqué the outer borders.

15. Trim all outer borders to 5¾″ from the outermost vine seamline.

16. Finish the quilt. (Refer to page 55 for instructions.)

Quilt Assembly Diagram

Quilts with a Spin

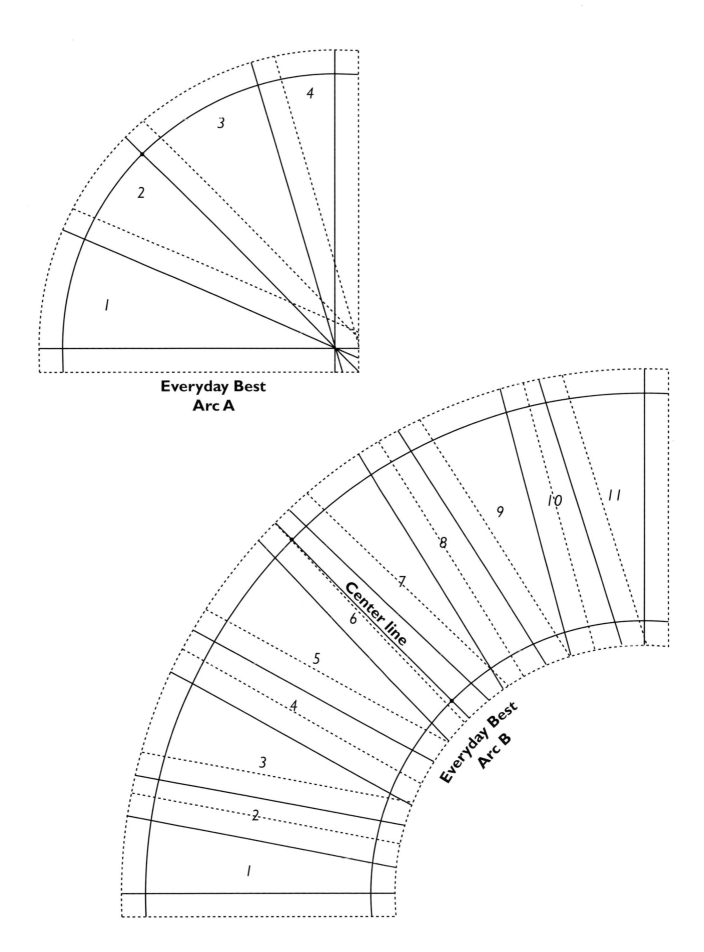

**Everyday Best
Arc A**

1
2
3
4

Center line

1
2
3
4
5
6
7
8
9
10
11

**Everyday Best
Arc B**

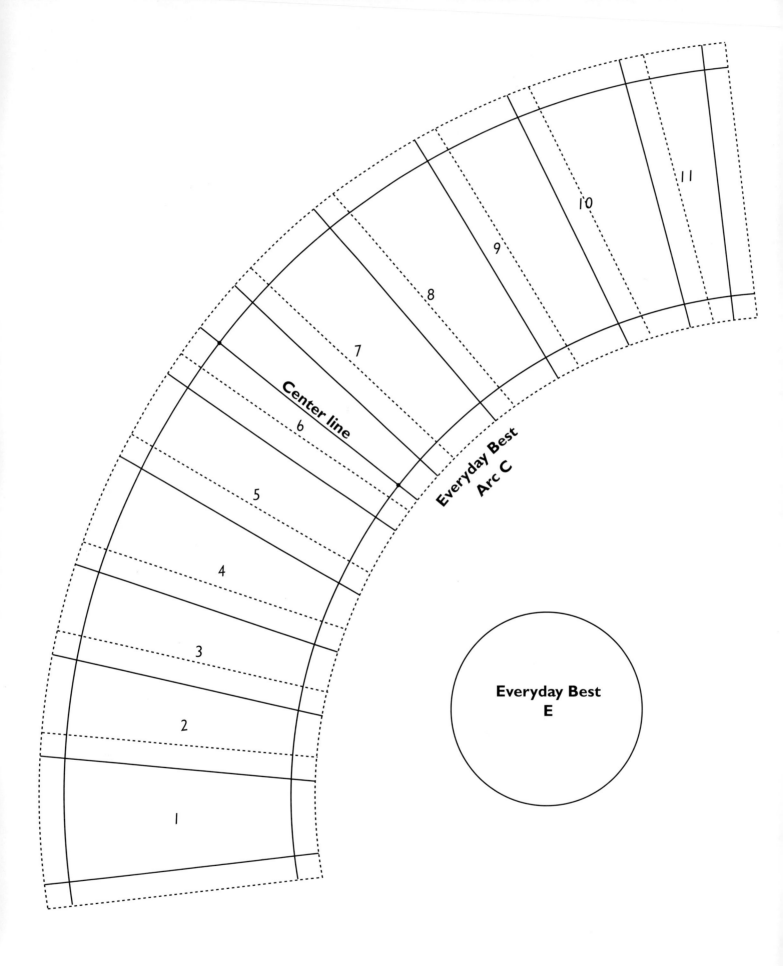

Center line

1

2

3

4

5

6

7

8

9

10

11

Everyday Best
Arc C

Everyday Best
E

Dresden Dots

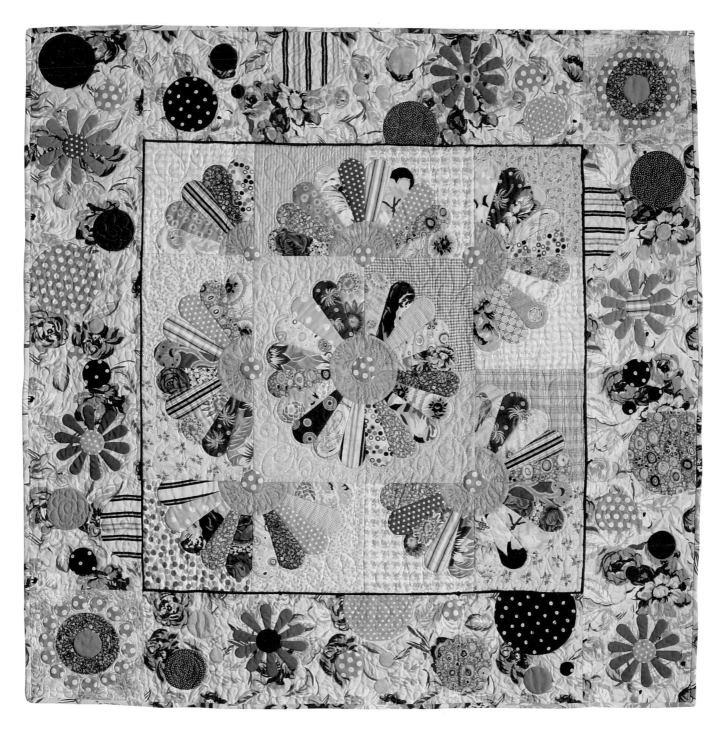

Made by Linda Jenkins, 2004

Quilted by Mary Covey

Finished quilt block: 8″ × 8″

Finished quilt size: 48″ × 48″

This is not your traditional Dresden Plate. Linda broke the plates apart, added some bubbly circles, and mixed it all with lots of color to make this very happy quilt.

Materials

This is a scrappy quilt. Use the yardage amounts below as a guide; they will vary with the number of fabrics you use.

Pink fabrics for block backgrounds: 1½ yards
Green floral fabric for border backgrounds: 1¼ yards
Fuchsia fabric for piping accent: ½ yard
Cotton cord for piping accent: 4 yards
Appliqué: A variety of bright fabric scraps to total approximately 3 yards
Backing and sleeve: 3 yards
Binding: ⅞ yard
Batting: 54″ × 54″

Cutting

Pink fabrics
Cut 18 squares 10″ × 10″.

Green floral fabric
Top and bottom borders: Cut 2 strips 10″ × 34″.
Side borders: Cut 2 strips 10″ × 42″.

Fuchsia fabric
Cut 1 square 14″ × 14″ to make a ¾″-wide continuous bias strip.

Binding
Cut 1 square 26″ × 26″ to make 2½″-wide continuous bias binding. (Refer to page 58 for instructions.)

Cut fabric for appliqué as needed.

Block Assembly

Dresden Plate Blocks

Refer to pages 52–54 for instructions on making the positioning overlay and preparing the appliqué.

1. Template A is finished size. Template B has a ¼″ seam allowance. Make 1 of each template.

2. Pierce template B through the 2 small dots, which indicate where the piece begins to curve.

3. On the wrong side of the plate fabric, trace around template B and place a mark through the pierced holes.

4. Cut out the fabric pieces just inside the drawn line.

5. On your design wall, arrange the plate pieces on the pink backgrounds. Move the pieces around until you are happy with their placement.

6. Choose a block. Place 2 adjacent plate pieces right sides together. Sew them together along the straight edge. At the mark where the curve begins, stop and backstitch. Repeat to make another pair. Press to one side.

7. Sew the remaining plate piece to the adjacent pair. Sew the 2 units together. Press to one side.

8. Place the plate unit right side up on a sandpaper board. Place template A over each piece in the plate, and trace around the outer curved edge of the template.

9. Finger-press the curved edges of the plate unit. Use the overlay to position the plate unit on a background. Pin or baste the unit in place. Appliqué the plate to the background along the outer curved edges.

10. Appliqué the center circle (template C). Press. Repeat for all blocks.

11. When your appliqué is complete, trim the blocks to 8½″ × 8½″. Trim away the background behind the plates.

12. Refer to the Quilt Assembly Diagram (page 40). Set the center of the quilt together. Press seams in alternate directions.

13. Appliqué circles C, D, and E where indicated over the seams. Be careful not to stretch the outer edges.

14. Make a continuous bias strip for the accent piping. (Refer to instructions on page 58.) Cut the strip 3/4″ wide and press it in half lengthwise, wrong sides together.

15. Cut 4 piping strips 32½″. Baste a piping strip to each side of the quilt. Sew it in place. Because only 1/8″ of this strip will show, it's important to be accurate in your sewing. Repeat for the top and bottom sides.

Border Assembly

1. Make border templates.

2. Make a pattern for the top border. Draw an 8″ × 32″ rectangle on a long piece of paper. Refer to the Quilt Assembly Diagram for appliqué shape placement in the top border. Place the templates on the paper and trace around them. Make your placement overlay from this pattern. Repeat for the bottom border.

3. Make patterns for the side borders in the same way. The rectangle size for the side border patterns is 8″ × 40″.

4. Place the border backgrounds on your design wall.

5. Audition all of the border appliqué pieces on the design wall. Remember to include the upper right and lower left border blocks.

6. Appliqué the borders.

7. When the appliqué is complete, press the borders on the wrong side.

8. Trim the top and bottom borders to 8½″ × 32½″.

9. Trim the side borders to 8½″ × 40½″.

10. Trim the upper right and lower left corner blocks to 8½″ × 8½″.

Quilt Assembly

Refer to the Quilt Assembly Diagram (page 40) for quilt construction.

1. Sew the top and bottom borders to the quilt. Press to the border.

2. Sew the lower left block to the left side border. Sew the border to the quilt. Press to the border.

3. Sew the upper right block to the right side border. Sew the border to the quilt. Press to the border.

4. Finish the quilt. (Refer to page 55 for instructions.)

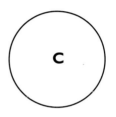

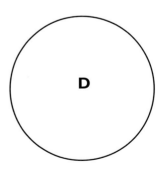

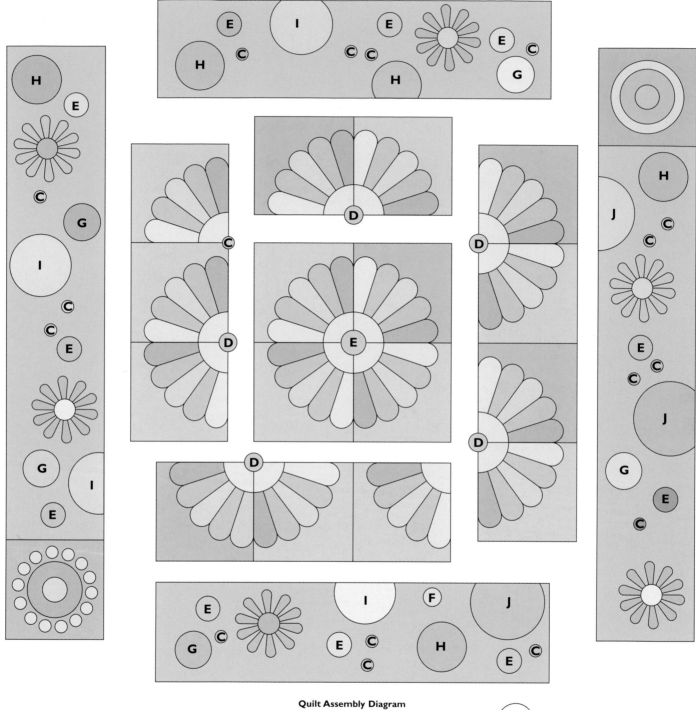

Quilt Assembly Diagram

Appliqué order for border flower.
*Patterns for appliqué borders are on the
pullouts at the back of the book.*

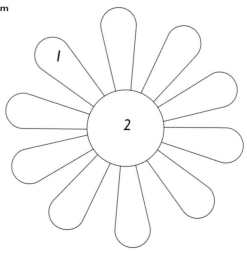

Quilts with a Spin

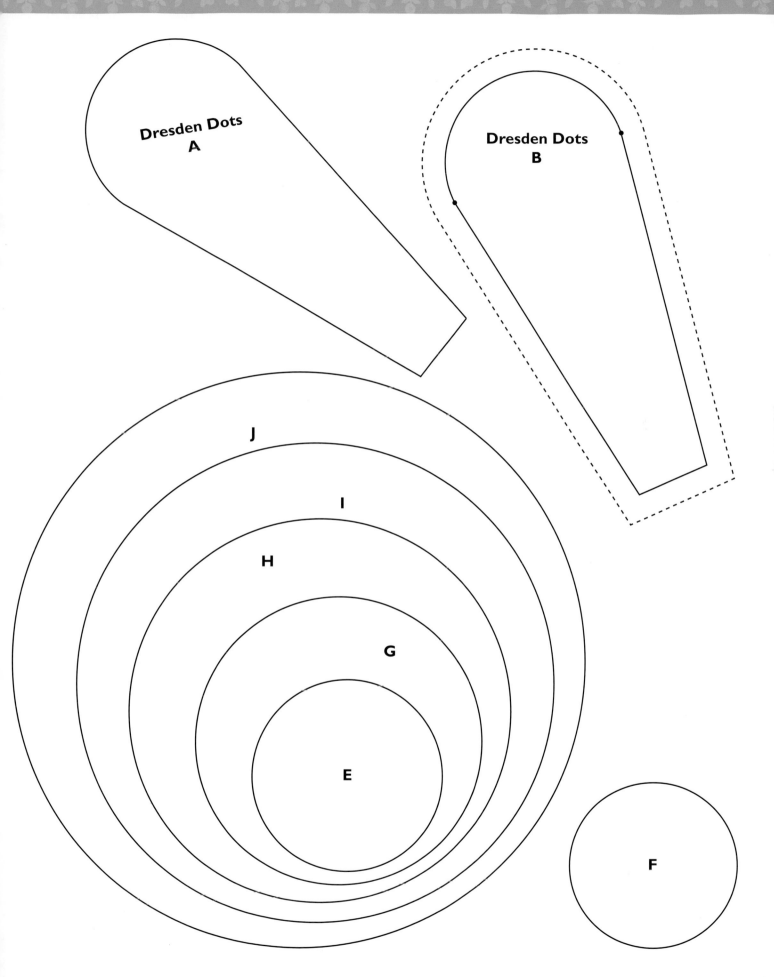

Dresden Dots
A

Dresden Dots
B

J

I

H

G

E

F

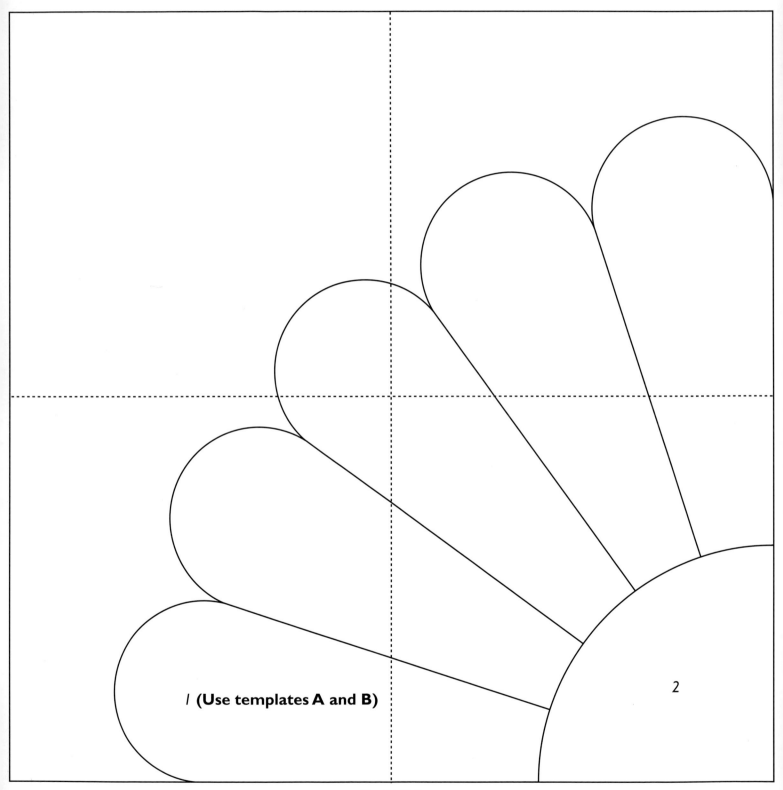

1 (Use templates A and B)

2

Dresden Dots
Full-size corner block
Trace to overlay.

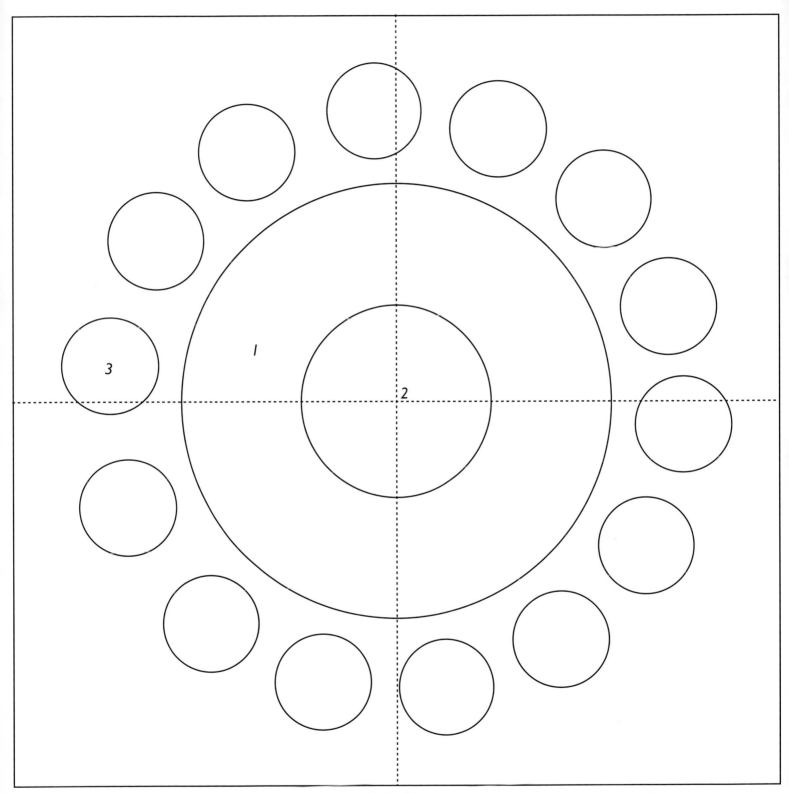

Dresden Dots
Full-size corner block
Trace to overlay.

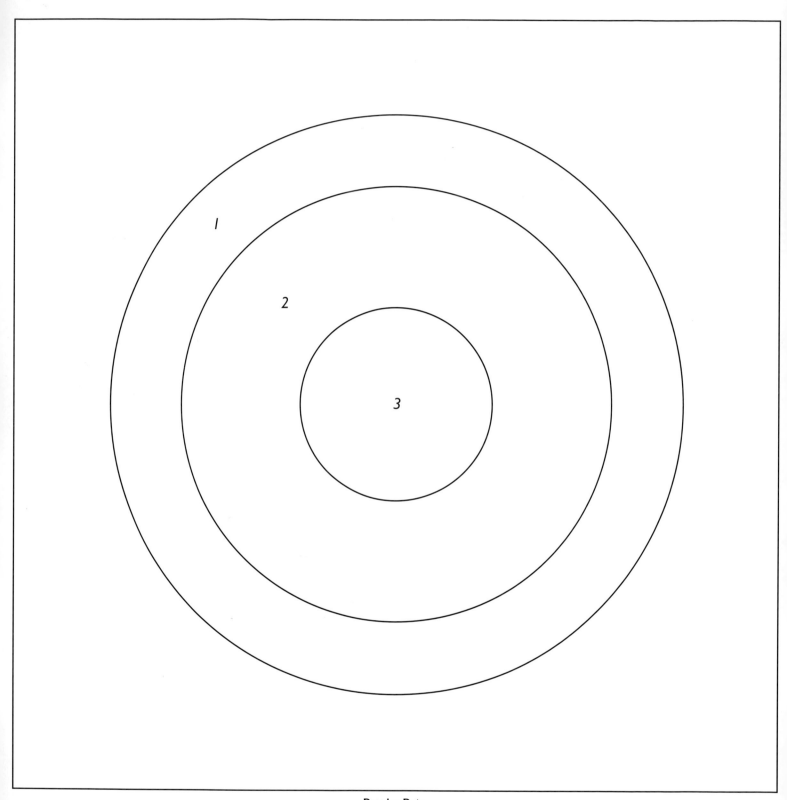

Dresden Dots
Full-size corner block
Trace to overlay.

Quilts with a Spin

Addicted to Dishes

Made by Becky Goldsmith, 2002

Finished appliqué block size: 5″ × 5″

Finished quilt size: 30″ × 30″

Becky loves dishes. Old dishes, new dishes, colorful dishes, elegant dishes—it doesn't matter; they are all good! The scrappy little blocks in this quilt are made from vibrant scraps of silk and a variety of man-made fibers. The elegance of these fibers makes these "dishes" a little more formal in feeling. Working on foundation papers made these slippery fabrics easier to handle.

Materials

This is a scrappy quilt. Use the yardage amounts below as a guide; they will vary with the number of fabrics you use.

Light fabric for block backgrounds: ⅝ yard
Dark fabric for block backgrounds: ¾ yard
Colorful fabric for pieced dishes: A variety to total 2½ yards
Dark fabric for corded binding: ⅝ yard
Cotton piping cord: 4½ yards
Backing and sleeve: 1¾ yards
Batting: 36″ × 36″

Cutting

Light fabric
Template B: Cut 16.
Template C: Cut 16.

Dark fabric
Template B: Cut 20.
Template C: Cut 20.

Colorful fabric
Cut 17 strips 4¼″ × 40″, then cut into 360 strips 1¾″ × 4¼″.
Template D: Cut 16.

Corded Binding
Cut 1 square 20″ × 20″ to make 2½″-wide continuous bias binding. (Refer to page 58 for instructions.)

Block Assembly

Refer to pages 52–54 for instructions on making the positioning overlay and preparing the appliqué.

Appliqué Tips

Use the *circle appliqué* technique for the circles at the center of the blocks. (Refer to pages 56–57 for instructions.)

Pieced Arcs

Refer to pages 60–61 for instructions on paper piecing the arcs. Refer to page 62 for instructions on sewing curves. Patterns for arcs C and B are on the pullouts at the back of the book.

1. Make 36 copies of arc foundation pattern A on vellum.

2. Cut out each copy, following the outer dashed lines.

3. Sew the arcs.

4. Use template B for 16 light block corners and 20 dark block corners. The darkest are to the outside of the quilt.

5. Use template C for 16 light block centers and 20 dark block centers. The darkest are to the outside of the quilt.

6. Use template D for the block centers.

7. Place the block arcs, corners, centers, and circles on your design wall. Move them around until you are happy with their placement. This is an important step—don't skip it!

8. Sew a B corner to its respective A arc. Always work with the concave side up. Press.

9. Carefully remove the paper from the arc.

10. Sew the A/B unit to the C block center. Pin as often as needed. Sew with the concave side up. Press.

11. Repeat for all arcs and corners.

Quilt Assembly

Refer to the Quilt Assembly Diagram (page 48) for quilt construction.

1. Sew 4 blocks together to make 1 complete center block. Press seams in alternate directions. Make 4 center blocks. Appliqué a circle D in the center of each block.

2. The sides of the quilt have 8 half-blocks. Sew blocks together into pairs. Press seams together in alternate directions. Appliqué one-half of a circle D on each half-block.

3. Appliqué one-quarter of a circle D on the remaining 4 corner blocks.

4. Sew the 4 center blocks together. Press in alternate directions.

5. Sew together the half-blocks for each side of the quilt. Sew them to the quilt. Press in alternate directions.

6. Sew together the half-blocks and corner blocks for the top of the quilt to form a row. Sew the row to the top of the quilt. Press in alternate directions. Repeat for the bottom row.

7. Finish the quilt. (Refer to page 55 for instructions.) Becky chose a corded binding for her quilt. (Refer to pages 58–59 for corded binding.) Regular bias binding will work as well.

Blocking Tips

Becky made her quilt from silk fabrics. Silk has a tendency to ripple so she used a steam iron to block the quilt into shape after quilting.

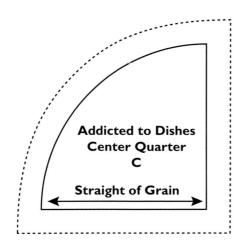

**Addicted to Dishes
Center Quarter
C**

Straight of Grain

D

**Addicted to Dishes
Center**

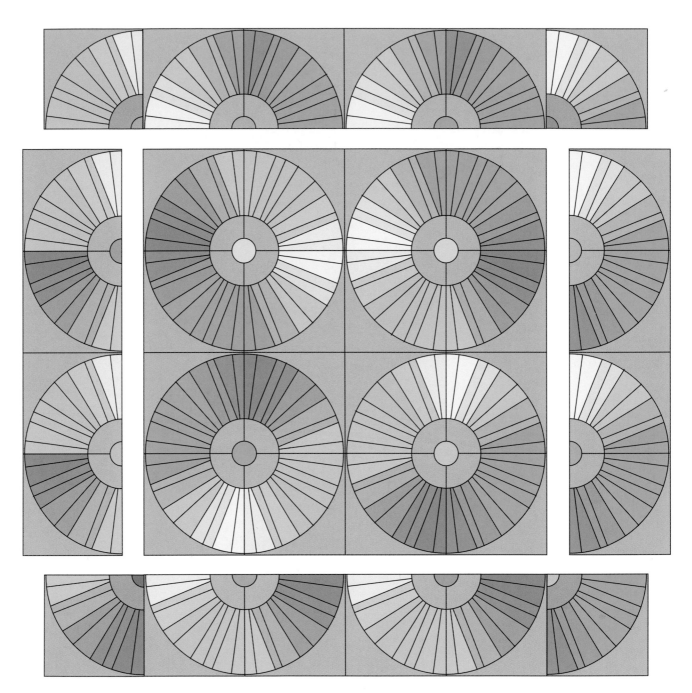

Quilt Assembly Diagram

Quilts with a Spin

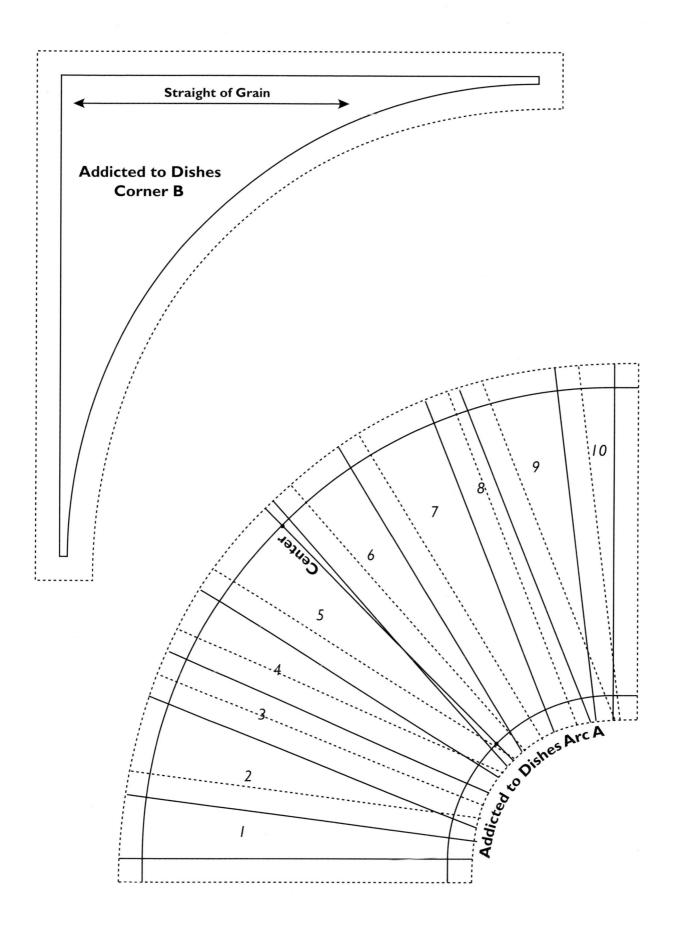

Straight of Grain

**Addicted to Dishes
Corner B**

Center

1

2

3

4

5

6

7

8

9

10

Addicted to Dishes Arc A

We have a great technique for appliqué that uses sturdy laminated appliqué templates and a clear vinyl positioning overlay, making it a snap to position all the pieces. If you're new to Piece O' Cake Designs appliqué techniques, read through this entire chapter before beginning a project.

For a more complete description of all of our appliqué techniques, refer to our book *The Appliqué Sampler*.

Preparing the Backgrounds for Appliqué

Always cut the background fabric larger than the size it will be when it is pieced into the quilt. The outer edges of the block can stretch and fray as you handle it while stitching. The appliqué can shift during stitching and cause the block to shrink slightly. For these reasons, it is best to add 1″ to all sides before cutting out the backgrounds. This amount is included in the cutting instructions for each quilt in this book. You will trim the blocks to size after you complete the appliqué.

1. Press each background block in half vertically and horizontally. This establishes a center grid in the background that will align with the center grid on the positioning overlay. When the backgrounds are pieced, the seamlines are the grid lines, so you do not need to press creases for centering.

Press to create a centering grid.

2. Use a pencil to draw a ¼″-long mark over each end of the pressed-in grid lines. Be sure not to make the marks too long or they will show on the block. These little lines make it easier to match up the overlay as you work with it and will help you find the center when trimming your block.

3. Use a pencil to draw a small × in *one corner* of the block background. This × will match up with an × that you draw on the overlay. Be sure to mark the × near the edge so it won't show on the finished block.

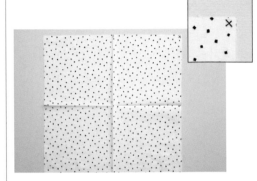

Making the Appliqué Templates

Each appliqué shape requires a template, and we have a unique way of making templates that is both easy and accurate.

1. Use a photocopier to make 2–5 copies of each block. If the patterns need to be enlarged, make the enlargement *before* making copies. Compare the copies with the original to be sure they are accurate.

2. Cut out groups of appliqué shapes from these copies. Leave a little paper allowance around each group. Where one shape overlaps another, cut the top shape from one copy and the bottom shape from another.

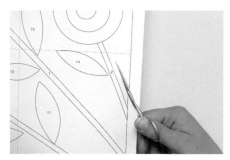

Cut out appliqué shapes.

3. Place a self-laminating sheet shiny side down on the table. Peel off the paper backing, leaving the sticky side of the sheet facing up.

4. If you are doing hand appliqué, place the templates *drawn* side down on the self-laminating sheet. For fusible appliqué, place the *blank* side down. Take care when placing each template onto the laminate. Use more laminating sheets as necessary.

For hand appliqué, place appliqué shapes *drawn* side down on self-laminating sheets.

For fusible appliqué, place appliqué shapes *blank* side down on self-laminating sheets.

5. Cut out each shape. Try to split the drawn line with your scissors—don't cut inside or outside the line. Keep edges smooth and points sharp.

Cut out each template.

Notice how easy it is to cut out these templates. That's the main reason we like this method. In addition, a mechanical copy of the pattern is more accurate than hand tracing onto template plastic. As you continue to use the templates, you'll see that they are sturdy and hold up to repeated use.

Some of the quilts in this book contain appliqué shapes that are bigger than a sheet of paper. You can still make templates using our technique. Simply make enough copies so that you have the entire shape on paper. Match the design and tape the copies together.

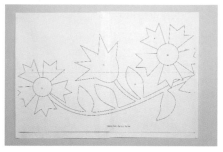

Tape copies together to make a large template.

Cover the template with pieces of laminate. It isn't necessary to butt the laminate pieces together; simply overlap them!

Cover the shape with pieces of laminate, overlapping the edges.

Using the Templates for Hand Appliqué

For needle-turn (hand) appliqué, the templates are used right side up on the right side of the fabric.

1. Place the appliqué fabric right side up on a sandpaper board.

2. Place the template right side up (shiny laminate side up) on the fabric so that as many edges as possible are on the diagonal grain of the fabric. A bias edge is easier to turn under than one on the straight of grain.

3. Trace around the template. The sandpaper will hold the fabric in place while you trace.

Place templates with as many edges as possible on the bias. Trace around each template.

4. Cut out each piece, adding a ³⁄₁₆″ turn-under allowance.

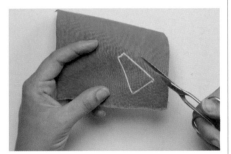

Cut out each piece, adding a ³⁄₁₆″ turn-under allowance.

5. Prepare all of the appliqué pieces for a block, then follow the instructions for Making the Positioning Overlay.

Using the Templates for Fusible Appliqué

For fusible appliqué, templates are used with the drawn side down (shiny laminate side up) on the wrong side of the fabric. Use a nonstick pressing cloth to protect the iron and ironing board.

We have reservations about recommending the use of fusible web. It is our opinion that this is not a good choice for an heirloom quilt. However, if you choose to use fusible web, follow the manufacturer's instructions. We also recommend that you stitch around the outside of all fused appliqué pieces either by hand or machine. A blanket stitch works well.

1. Follow the manufacturer's instructions and iron the fusible web to the *wrong* side of the appliqué fabric. Do not peel off the paper backing.

Iron fusible web to the *wrong* side of fabric.

2. Leave the fabric right side down. Place the template drawn side down (shiny laminate side up), and trace around it onto the paper backing of the fusible web.

Trace around template onto paper backing.

3. Cut out the appliqué pieces on the drawn line. Add a scant ³⁄₁₆″ allowance to any part of an appliqué piece that lies under another piece.

Cut out appliqué pieces on drawn line.

4. Prepare all of the appliqué pieces for a block, then follow the instructions for Making the Positioning Overlay.

Making the Positioning Overlay

The positioning overlay is a piece of medium-weight clear upholstery vinyl that is used to accurately position each appliqué piece on the block. The overlay is easy to make and use, and it makes your projects portable.

1. Cut a piece of the upholstery vinyl, including its tissue paper lining, to the finished size of each block. Set the tissue paper aside until you are ready to fold or store the overlay.

2. Make a copy of the patterns in this book to work from. If indicated, enlarge the pattern before copying. Tape pattern pieces together as needed.

3. Tape the pattern copy onto a table.

4. Tape the upholstery vinyl over the pattern. Use a ruler and a Sharpie Ultra Fine Point marker to draw the pattern's horizontal and vertical centerlines onto the vinyl.

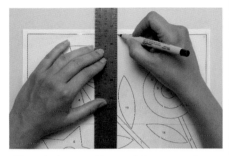
Tape vinyl over pattern and draw centerlines.

5. Accurately trace all the lines from the pattern onto the vinyl. The numbers on the pattern indicate the stitching sequence— include these numbers on the overlay.

6. Draw a small × in one corner of the placement overlay.

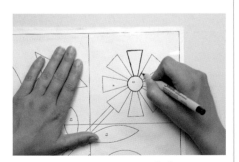
Trace pattern onto vinyl.

Using the Positioning Overlay for Hand Appliqué

1. Place the background right side up on the work surface. We like to work on top of our sandpaper board because the sandpaper keeps the background from shifting.

2. Place the overlay right side up on top of the background.

3. Line up either the center grid of the fabric or the seamlines with the center grid of the overlay. Place the × on the overlay in the same corner as the × on the block.

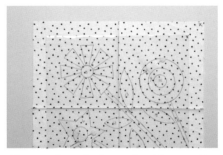
Place overlay on background and line up grids.

4. If necessary, pin the overlay to keep it from shifting out of position.

5. Before placing appliqué pieces on the block, finger-press the turn-under allowances. **This is a very important step.** As you finger-press, make sure that the drawn line is pressed to the back. You'll be amazed at how much easier this step makes needle-turning the turn-under allowance.

Finger-press each piece, with the drawn line to the back.

6. Place the appliqué piece under the overlay but on top of the background. It is easy to tell when the appliqué pieces are in position under the overlay. As you work, finger-press and position one piece at a time. Be sure to follow the appliqué order.

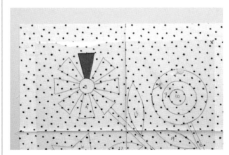
Use overlay to position appliqué pieces.

7. Fold back the overlay, and pin the appliqué pieces in place using ½″ sequin pins. You can pin against the sandpaper board; doing so does not dull the pins. We usually position and stitch only one or two pieces at a time. Remove the vinyl overlay before stitching.

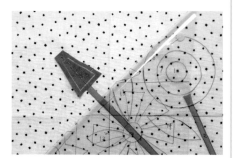

Pin the appliqué piece in place.

8. Hand appliqué the pieces in place with an invisible stitch and matching thread.

9. When you are ready to put away the overlay, place the saved tissue paper over the drawn side before folding it. The tissue paper keeps the lines from transferring from one part of the vinyl to another.

For Your Information

We don't trim the fabric behind our appliqué. We believe that leaving the background intact makes the quilt stronger. Also, should the quilt ever need to be repaired, it's easier if the background has not been cut.

Using the Positioning Overlay for Fusible Appliqué

1. Place the background right side up on the ironing board.

2. Place the overlay right side up on top of the background.

3. Line up either the center grid of the fabric or the seamlines with the center grid of the overlay.

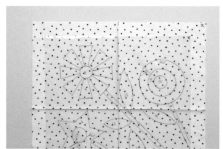

Place overlay on background and line up grids.

4. Peel off the paper backing from each appliqué piece as you go. Be careful not to stretch or ravel the outer edges.

5. Place the appliqué pieces right side up, under the overlay but on top of the background. Start with appliqué piece 1 and follow the appliqué order. It is easy to tell when the appliqué pieces are in position under the overlay. You may be able to position several pieces at once.

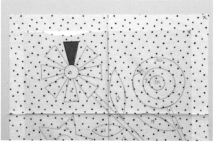

Use overlay to position appliqué pieces.

6. Carefully remove the overlay. Iron the appliqué pieces in place. Be sure to follow the manufacturer's instructions for your brand of fusible web. Do not touch the overlay vinyl with the iron because the vinyl will melt.

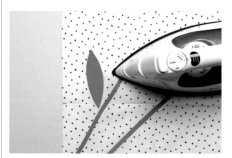

Fuse appliqué pieces in place.

7. After fusing cotton fabric, we sew the raw edges of the fused appliqué by hand or on the sewing machine, using matching thread and a straight or blanket stitch. This keeps the edges secure as the quilts are used.

Pressing and Trimming the Blocks

1. After you complete the appliqué, press the blocks on the wrong side. If the ironing surface is hard, place the blocks on a towel to keep the appliqué from getting flattened. Be careful not to stretch the blocks as you press.

2. Carefully trim each block to size. Measure from the center out, and always use a ruler to make sure the design is properly aligned before you cut off the excess fabric.

Finishing the Quilt

1. Assemble the quilt top according to the instructions for each project.

2. Construct the back of the quilt, piecing as needed.

3. Place the backing right side down on a firm surface. Tape it down to keep it from moving while you baste.

4. Place the batting over the backing and pat out any wrinkles.

5. Center the quilt top right side up over the batting.

6. Baste the layers together. Yes, we hand baste for both hand and machine quilting.

7. Quilt by hand or machine.

8. Trim the outer edges. Allow ¼"–⅜" of backing and batting to extend beyond the edge of the quilt top. This extra fabric and batting will fill the binding nicely.

Trim outer edges.

9. Finish the outer edges with continuous bias binding. (Refer to instructions on pages 58–60.)

Making a Label and Sleeve

1. Make a hanging sleeve and attach it to the back of the quilt.

2. Make a label and sew it to the back of the quilt. Include information you want people to know about the quilt, such as your name and address, the date, the fiber content of the quilt and batting, and whether the quilt was made for a special person or occasion.

Special Techniques

Cutaway Appliqué

The cutaway technique makes it much easier to stitch irregular, long, thin, or very small pieces. It is especially good to use for stems, the whirlygig blades, the empress feathers, stars, and the zigzag border in the *Pennsylvania Pickle Dish*.

1. Place the template on top of the selected fabric. Be sure to place the template on the fabric so that most of the edges are on the diagonal grain of the fabric. Trace around the template.

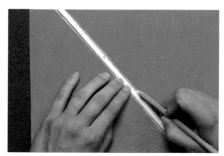

Place template with as many edges as possible on the bias. Trace template.

2. Cut out the appliqué piece, leaving 1″ or more of excess fabric around the traced shape. Leave fabric intact in the V between points, inside deep curves, and so on.

3. Finger-press, making sure the drawn line is pressed to the back.

4. Use the vinyl placement overlay to position the appliqué piece on the block.

5. Place pins ¼″ from the finger-pressed edge. Place pins parallel to the edges. Large pieces, such as the whirlygig center, can be basted in place. First pin the shape in place, then baste it. When a shape is curved, sew the concave side first, if possible.

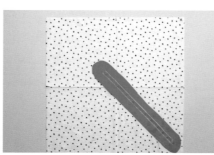

Pin the appliqué piece in place. Baste large shapes if you prefer.

6. Begin trimming the excess fabric from where you will start stitching, leaving a ³⁄₁₆″ turn-under allowance. Never start stitching at an inner or outer point that will be turned under.

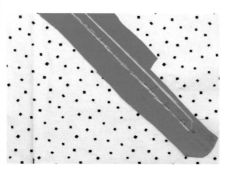

Trim excess fabric and begin stitching.

7. Trim more fabric as you sew. Clip inner curves and inner points as needed.

8. Remove the pins as you stitch the next side of the piece. Trim excess fabric as necessary.

9. Continue until all sides of the appliqué piece are stitched.

Circle Appliqué

When sewing outer curves and circles, you can control only one stitch at a time. Use the needle or a round wooden toothpick to smooth out any pleats that form. Remember, the more you practice, the better you'll get.

1. Trace circles onto the selected fabric. Cut out each circle, adding a ³⁄₁₆″ turn-under allowance.

2. Finger-press the turn-under allowance, making sure the drawn line is pressed to the back.

3. Use the vinyl overlay to position the appliqué piece. Pin it in place. Use at least 2 pins to keep the circle from shifting.

4. Begin sewing. Turn under only enough turn-under allowance to take 1 or 2 stitches. If you turn under more than that, the appliqué will have flat spaces and points.

Turn under only enough for 1 or 2 stitches.

5. Use the tip of the needle or a toothpick to reach under the appliqué to spread open any folds and to smooth out any points.

As seen from back. Use needle to open folds and to smooth points.

6. To close the circle, turn under the last few stitches all at once. The circle will tend to flatten out.

7. Use the tip of the needle to smooth out the pleats in the turn-under allowance and to pull the flattened part of the circle into a rounded shape.

Finish stitching circle.

Off-the-Block Construction

It is sometimes easier to sew appliqué pieces off the block and then sew them as a unit to the block. Use this technique when appliqué pieces are stacked one on top of the other, as in flower 11/12/13 in the borders of *Whirlygig*.

1. Choose the fabrics for the appliqué. Trace around the templates onto the respective fabrics. Cut out the appliqué pieces, leaving enough excess fabric so the pieces are easy to hold on to.

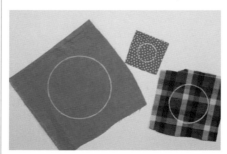

Trace and cut appliqué pieces.

2. In off-the-block construction, you work from the top down. Cut out the top piece, leaving a ³/₁₆″ turn-under allowance. Finger-press the piece, and position it over the second-from-the-top piece. Pin the top piece in place, and sew it down.

Work from the top down.

3. Trim the excess fabric from the newly created unit, leaving a ³/₁₆″ seam allowance. Finger-press the piece, and position it over the next piece down. Pin the combined unit in place, and sew it down.

Trim excess, position over the next piece, and sew.

4. Trim the excess fabric from the unit, leaving a ³/₁₆″ turn-under allowance. The entire piece is now ready to be finger-pressed and positioned on the block.

Making Continuous Bias Binding

We find this method for making continuous bias to be particularly easy. A surprisingly small amount of fabric makes quite a bit of bias, and there is no waste. We also show you how to master those tricky binding corners on pages 59–60.

We normally make our bindings 2½″ wide.

1. Start with a square of fabric and cut it in half diagonally. Refer to the project instructions for the size of the square.

2. Sew the two triangles together, right sides together. Be sure to sew the edges that are on the straight of grain. If you are using striped fabric, match the stripes. You may need to offset the fabric a little to make the stripes match.

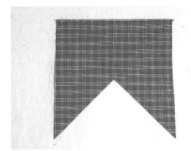

Sew triangle's straight-of-grain edges together.

3. Press the seam allowances open. Make a short cut 2½″ wide into each side.

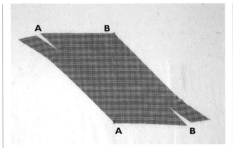

Make a short cut 2½″ wide.

4. Match the A's and B's, with the fabric right sides together making a tube. Pin and sew. Press the seam open.

Pin and sew. Press.

5. Use a rotary cutter and ruler to cut the continuous bias strip 2½″ wide.

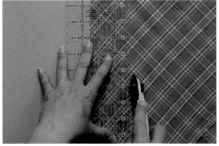

Cut to desired width.

6. Press the length of bias strip wrong sides together for double-fold binding.

Continuous Bias Cutting Tip

Try putting a small cutting mat on the end of the ironing board. Slide the tube of fabric over the mat. Use a ruler and rotary cutter to cut a long strip of continuous bias, rotating the tube of fabric as needed. Cut using gentle pressure. If the ironing board is padded, the cutting surface may give if you press very hard.

Corded Binding

Cording is sewn to the quilt top before it is layered and quilted.

1. Make a strip of continuous bias binding, as described above. Cut the strip 2″ wide for cording.

2. Press the strip *gently* in half lengthwise, wrong sides together.

3. Cut the first end of the bias strip at a 45° angle. Turn under this end ½″ and press.

4. Place ¼″ cotton piping cord down the lengthwise fold of the bias strip, 1½″ from the first end of the strip.

Place cotton piping cord down the center of the bias strip.

5. Using a zipper foot, sew the piping cord into the bias strip.

6. Trim excess fabric, leaving a ¼″ seam allowance. **Do not trim excess fabric at the first end of the strip**; you'll want to be able to hold this fabric when you hide the end of the cord.

Trim excess fabric, leaving a ¼″ seam allowance. Do not trim excess fabric at the first end of the strip.

7. With raw edges even, pin the cording to the edge of the quilt top, beginning a few inches from a corner. Start sewing 2″ from the beginning of the cording strip, using a ¼″ seam allowance. Your corners will be rounded. Make sure that all corners have the same degree of roundness.

8. Work your way around the quilt. When you get back to the beginning, cut the cording so that it is even with the end of the cord

at the first end. Nestle the cut end inside the first end of the cording. Sew it in place. Cut off the excess fabric.

9. Layer, baste, and quilt. Stop quilting just before you reach the edge of the quilt.

10. Trim the batting even with the cording seamline. Cut the backing even with the raw edges of the top and cording.

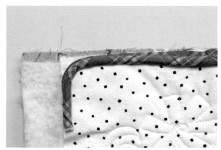

Trim the batting even with the cording seamline. Cut the backing even with the raw edges of the top and cording.

11. Turn the top and cording seam allowances over the edge of the batting. Turn under the backing seam allowance and invisibly stitch it in place.

Turn the top and cording seam allowances over the batting edge. Turn under the backing seam allowance and invisibly stitch in place.

12. Finish quilting.

Sewing Binding to the Quilt

1. Cut the first end of the binding at a 45° angle. Turn under this end ½″ and press.

2. Press the continuous binding strip in half lengthwise, wrong sides together.

3. With raw edges even, pin the binding to the edge of the quilt, beginning a few inches from a corner. Start sewing 6″ from the beginning of the binding strip, using a ¼″ seam allowance.

4. Stop ¼″ from the corner and backstitch several stitches.

Stop ¼″ from corner. Backstitch.

5. Fold the binding straight up. Note the 45° angle.

Fold binding up.

6. Fold the binding straight down and begin sewing the next side of the quilt.

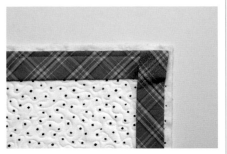

Fold binding down and begin sewing.

7. Sew the binding to all sides of the quilt, following the process in Steps 3–4. Stop a few inches before the beginning of the binding, but don't trim the excess binding yet.

8. Overlap the ends of the binding and cut the second end at a 90° angle. *Be sure to cut the binding long enough so the cut end is covered completely by the angled end.*

9. Slip the 90° end into the angled end.

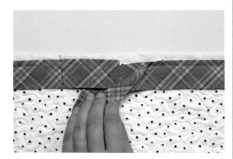

Slip 90° end into angled end.

10. Pin the joined ends to the quilt and finish sewing the binding to the quilt.

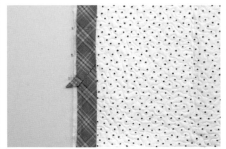

Pin and finish sewing.

11. Turn the binding to the back of the quilt, covering the raw edges. If there is too much batting, trim some to leave your binding nicely filled. Hand stitch the folded edge of the binding to the back of the quilt.

Paper Piecing

Paper piecing is a great way to do very accurate piecing. It is especially suited to the pieced arcs in several of the quilts in this book. Always sew with the printed side of the paper up, facing you. Fabric is placed on the unprinted side of the paper.

We prefer to use vellum when paper piecing, because it is a crisp, translucent paper that allows you to see what you are doing. It is also easier to remove than plain paper. Try it. You'll like it!

1. Photocopy or trace onto vellum the number of paper piecing patterns needed for the project. Compare the copies to the original to be certain that you have accurate copies. Trim papers along the outer dashed edge of the pattern.

2. Use a strong, fine, cotton thread for paper piecing. We use the same thread that we use for appliquéing.

3. Sew the fabric to the vellum, using a large needle (size 90/14) in the sewing machine. Use a shorter-than-normal stitch length—18–20 stitches per inch or 1.5–1.8. This results in tighter stitches that can't be pulled apart when you remove the paper.

4. Start sewing at the #1 end of the pattern. Place the first two pieces of fabric right sides together on the unprinted side of the vellum. Make sure that the wrong side of the first piece of fabric is next to the vellum.

Line up the edges of the fabric with the *dashed line* on the paper. Sew on the *solid line*. Always sew with the drawn lines up and the fabric underneath, next to the feed dogs.

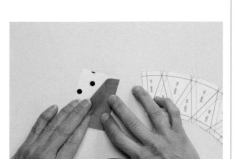

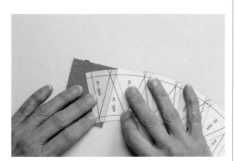

Place 2 fabric strips right sides together beneath the paper at the #1 position. Sew on the solid line.

5. Press open. The pattern is marked to indicate where the light and dark fabrics should be. Check that your fabrics are where they are supposed to be.

Press open.

6. Fold back the paper along the next dashed line and trim the excess fabric. Be careful not to cut the paper.

Fold back the paper and trim.

7. Carefully place the next strip. Be sure that, when sewn and pressed open, the strip will completely cover the next area. Sew it in place, press, and trim. Proceed in this manner until the entire strip is covered.

8. To finish, trim any fabric that sticks out beyond the edge of the paper.

Finish by trimming all excess fabric.

9. Remove the paper when indicated by the pattern.

Paper Piecing Tips

Use finer thread when sewing to paper. We use the same machine-embroidery thread that we use in our hand appliqué. (Refer to Supplies on page 5.) Clean your sewing machine often, as bits of paper tend to gather in the bobbin area.

Curved Piecing

Sewing a curve is easy. Always sew with the concave side up. Pin wisely. Follow our instructions, and you won't go wrong.

1. Fold the concave piece in half. Finger-press the center.

Finger-press the center of the concave piece.

2. The center is marked on the paper pieced arcs. With right sides together, pin the center of the concave side to the center of the arc.

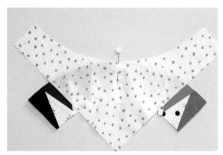

Match the centers, and pin.

3. Match the right end of the concave side to the right end of the arc. Pin these ends together.

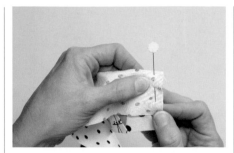

Pin the right ends together.

4. Match the left end of the concave side to the left end of the arc. Pin these ends together.

Pin the left ends together.

5. Sew the two pieces together. Carefully move the concave edge into position as you sew.

Sew the corner to the arc. Carefully move the concave edge of the corner into position as you sew.

6. Press the seams to the least bulky side.

Press seams to the least bulky side.

About the Authors

The Green Country Quilter's Guild in Tulsa, Oklahoma can be credited for bringing Linda Jenkins and Becky Goldsmith together. Their friendship developed while they worked together on many guild projects, and through a shared love for appliqué. This partnership led to the birth of Piece O' Cake Designs in 1994, and survived Linda's move to Pagosa Springs, Colorado, and then back to Tulsa in 2001, while Becky headed for Sherman, Texas.

Linda owned and managed a beauty salon before she started quilting. Over the years she developed a fine eye for color as a hair colorist and makeup artist. Becky's degree in interior design and many art classes provided a perfect background for quilting. Linda and Becky have shown many quilts, and have won numerous awards. Together they make a dynamic quilting duo, and love to teach other quilters the joys of appliqué.

In the fall of 2002 Becky and Linda joined the C&T Publishing family, where they continue to produce wonderful books and patterns.

For more informtion about individual Piece O' Cake patterns, contact C&T Publishing.

Index

Useful Information

Projects

Resources

For More Information

Ask for a free catalog:

C&T Publishing, Inc.
P.O. Box 1456
Lafayette, CA 94549
800-284-1114
email: ctinfo@ctpub.com
website: www.ctpub.com

Resources

Piece O' Cake Designs
website: www.pieceocake.com

Sewing Machines

Bernina of America
website: www. Berninausa.com

Office Supplies

(Self-laminating sheets)
Viking Office Supplies
website: www.viking.com
800-711-4242

Quilting Supplies

Cotton Patch Mail Order
3404 Hall Lane
Dept CTB
Lafayette, CA 94549
800-835-4418 925-283-7883
email: quiltusa@yahoo.com
website: www.quiltusa.com

Note: Fabrics used in the quilts shown may not be currently available, as fabric manufacturers keep most fabrics in print for only a short time.